Computer Langua

CW01510624

Assem Language for the 80286

Robert Erskine

Pitman

Consultant Editor: David Hatter

PITMAN PUBLISHING LIMITED
128 Long Acre, London WC2E 9AN

Associated Companies
Pitman Publishing Pty Ltd, Melbourne
Pitman Publishing New Zealand Ltd, Wellington
Copp Clark Pitman, Toronto

First edition 1985

British Library Cataloguing in Publication Data

Erskine, Robert
   Assembly Language for the 80286.—(Computer handbooks)
   1. INTEL 80286 (Microprocessor)—Programming
   2. Assembler language (Computer program language)
   I. Title   II. Series
001.64′24   QA76.8.1291/

ISBN 0 273 02391 8

Printed in Great Britain at The Bath Press, Avon

Contents

How to Use this Handbook

This Handbook is intended for the general programmer rather than for the systems design specialist and is centred on the Intel 80286 programming instruction set, data organization and addressing capabilities rather than on technical aspects of operating functions or on circuit design.

Although readers need not have prior knowledge of the Intel 16-bit series or of other 16-bit microprocessors, it would be helpful to have some understanding of the principles of assembly language programming. Special terms and concepts relating specifically to the Intel series are explained in the text but common terms which are used in assembly language programming, such as interrupts and stacks, are assumed to be reasonably familiar to the reader.

The book covers the system architecture of the 80286 and explains addressing modes in some detail. Features such as interrupts and I/O are also included, together with outlines of the multi-tasking, virtual memory management and protection mechanisms of the processor. The main part of the Handbook consists of a complete glossary of programming instructions, with descriptions of the operational functions of all types of commands and their variants.

The Intel 80286

The Intel 80286, known also as the iAPX 286, is an
advanced development of the 8086 processor,
which extends the range of the iAPX series to
include real-time, multi-user, multi-tasking
capabilities and powerful memory management and
protection facilities. It is also instruction set
compatible with the 8086/88, permitting the use of
existing applications software.

The 80286 is significantly faster than the 8086,
giving as much as a six-fold improvement in
execution time, and is capable of supporting more
than fifteen simultaneous users. This enhanced
performance is mainly the result of the division of
the processor into four, separate, pipelined,
functional units which operate in parallel and which
control the bus, the code translation and the
execution and memory management functions of
the system.

The four units operate as follows:

The bus unit functions as a communications
interface between the CPU, memory and I/O
systems and checks internal and external requests. It
contains an instruction prefetch mechanism which
loads up to six bytes of instruction data to a
prefetch queue while an earlier instruction is still
being processed.

The instruction unit collects instructions from the
prefetch queue, translates them and passes them to
its own instruction queue to await execution.

The execution unit contains the CPU registers and ALU and processes the decoded instructions passed from the instruction unit in response to a 'ready' signal issued by the ROM.

The address unit controls the memory management and protection functions of the system, mapping virtual memory to physical address space and checking requests from tasks against access rights data stored in internal register extensions.

The addressing range of the 80286 is also significantly greater, with an addressable physical memory space of 16 megabytes and the capacity to provide up to one gigabyte of virtual memory space for each user. On start-up, the processor provides a 20-bit real addressing capability, identical to that of the 8086 and 8088, while in protected virtual addressing mode, the addressing capability is extended to 24 bits, giving a sixteen-fold increase in directly addressable memory.

Data Lengths

The four main data types supported by the Intel processors are of 1, 4, 8 and 16-bit lengths, designated as bit, nibble (4-bit binary-coded decimal) and signed and unsigned byte and word lengths respectively. In some instances, for example where the quotient and remainder of a division operation total 32 bits, the extended data is split and stored as two word-sized lengths. Binary-coded decimal numbers may be stored as packed or unpacked values in the ranges $0-99$ and $0-9$ respectively. In the latter case the four most significant bits of the BCD byte are reset.

Signed 32- and 64-bit integers and signed 32-, 64- and 80-bit floating point values are supported in configurations using the iAPX 286/20 numeric data processor, which is an 80286 configured with an 80287 numeric processor extension.

20- and 24-bit real address specifications are special cases and are calculated internally by the system.

Real and Protected Modes

The 80286 operates in two modes: *real address mode* and *protected virtual address mode* (normally referred to as *protected mode*).

Real address mode is the default mode and is effective on power-up. In most respects this mode corresponds to the standard 8086/88 operating mode, except that in operation it is up to six times faster. All 8086/88 programs can be run unmodified in real mode and the range of addressable memory is identical (1 megabyte).

Protected mode, which is initialized by setting the PE flag in the machine status register, extends the addressable resident memory to 16 megabytes and permits access to up to one gigabyte (2^{30} bytes) of virtual address space per user. In protected mode, the address space allocated to each user, and to each task, is fully protected by a memory management system and the operating system, which is a global resource available to all applications programs, is protected by a hierarchical privilege system. These aspects of the protected operating mode will be described in greater detail in later sections of the Handbook.

As is the case with real address mode, applications programs written for the 8086/88 may also be run in protected mode, and the address translation required for addressing the larger memory space is handled automatically by the system.

Note that in order to protect the multi-user, multi-tasking environment from interference by applications programs, the selection of protected mode is irreversible and it can only be terminated by a complete system reset or by shutting off the power.

Sources and Destinations

The terms 'source' and 'destination' are used
throughout this book to distinguish the status of the
operands specified by instructions. In the case of
the programming instruction **MOV AX,BX** for
example, BX is designated the source operand and
AX the destination operand. Effectively, the
instruction means that data contained in the source
operand, to the right of the comma, is to be moved
into the destination operand to the left of the
comma. This is the opposite of the format used with
some other processors, such as the Motorola
68000, where the source and destination operands
are expressed in reverse order.

Segmentation

The directly addressable memory space available to
a task at any given time is divided into four 64K
segments: the *code segment*, containing the
instruction codes; the *data segment*, containing
program data; the *stack segment* and the *extra
segment*, which is used as an additional data area.
   In real address mode the current base address of
each segment is held in special 16-bit pointer
registers termed *segment registers*. Any 20-bit
address within the system is automatically computed
by multiplying the appropriate segment register by
16 and adding offset values, which may be either
constants or the contents of other registers.

In protected mode a 24-bit segment base address is used and each segment register is provided with a hidden extension cache which contains the segment base address and additional memory management information.

The segment registers are described in greater detail in the following section.

Register Model

The 80286 has seven groups of registers: the data registers, the pointer and index registers, the segment registers, the status and control registers and the task and local descriptor table registers, all of which are 16 bits in length; and the explicit cache registers, which are invisible to programs and which contain memory management data associated with the segment and system registers. The cache registers are up to 48 bits in length as indicated in the diagrams below.

Data registers:

AH	AL	AX: Accumulator
BH	BL	BX: Base
CH	CL	CX: Count
DH	DL	DX: Data

Pointer and index registers:

15	0	SP: Stack pointer
15	0	BP: Base pointer
15	0	SI: Source index
15	0	DI: Destination index

Segment registers:

15	0	
15	0	CS: Code segment
15	0	DS: Data segment
15	0	SS: Stack segment
15	0	ES: Extra segment

Status and control registers:

15	0	
15	0	IP: Instruction pointer
15	0	MSW: Machine status word
15	0	FLAGS: Flags register

Task and descriptor table registers:

15	0	
15	0	TR: Task register
15	0	LDTR: Local descriptor table register

Segment descriptor cache registers:

ACCESS		BASE ADDR		SEG.SIZE		
7	0	23	0	15	0	CS cache
7	0	23	0	15	0	DS cache
7	0	23	0	15	0	SS cache
7	0	23	0	15	0	ES cache

Task descriptor cache registers:

ACCESS		BASE ADDR		SEG.SIZE		
7	0	23	0	15	0	TR cache
7	0	23	0	15	0	LDTR cache
		23	0	15	0	GDTR cache
		23	0	15	0	IDTR cache

General data registers

Each of the data registers, AX, BX, CX and DX, may be used as 16-bit or as two separate 8-bit registers, hence their sub-division into eight separately identifiable bytes labelled AH to DH and AL to DL; the 'H' and the 'L' referring to their status as 'high' or 'low' bytes when used as word length registers. Although the data registers are mainly used straightforwardly for 8- and 16-bit arithmetic, for logical operations and for data transfer, in some circumstances they are assigned specific functions, as follows:

AX (Accumulator)
The AX register functions as the 'accumulator' and as such is involved in specific types of operations such as IN (data input), OUT (data output), XLAT (translation), multiplication, division, decimal adjustment and binary-coded decimal operations.

BX (Base)
The BX register is frequently used as a base register for referencing memory locations. In these cases BX holds the base address of a table or array in which specific locations are referenced by adding an offset value.

CX (Counter)

CX functions as a 16-bit counter register for counting the number of bytes or words in a specific string of data during string operations and in looping operations. For example, if n words are to be moved from one memory area to another, CX would initially hold the total number of words to be moved and is used to count off each word or byte as it is transferred. CL is used as an 8-bit counter for shift and rotation instructions.

DX (Data)

DX is used in multiplication operations to hold part of a 32-bit product, or in division operations to hold a remainder value. It may also be used in IN and OUT operations to specify the address of the I/O port being used.

Pointer and index registers

The pointer and index registers are used to hold offset values for accessing certain commonly used memory locations, such as the location of the top of the stack or blocks of data within a segment such as arrays and individual records.

The two 'pointer' registers, SP and BP, are used to hold offsets within the current stack segment of memory while the two 'index' registers, SI and DI, are used to contain offsets within the current data segment of memory. On some occasions there are exceptions to these general rules, for example where data is being transferred from one location to another, with the source and destination locations being indicated by SI and DI respectively.

An important feature of all four registers in this group is that they may be used in arithmetical and logical operations, thus enabling the offset values contained in them to be the results of prior computations.

SP
SP is the 'stack pointer' which points to the location of the top of the machine stack (i.e. the current stack segment). The stack pointer is the register implicitly used by the PUSH and POP instructions which store and retrieve data from the stack.

BP
BP is a 'base pointer', which points to an area within the stack which is allocated as a data storage area.

SI
SI is the 'source index' register which is used as an index register in certain indirect addressing modes. It is also used to contain an offset to address the location of a source operand during string operations.

DI
DI is the 'destination index' register which is used as an index register in certain indirect addressing modes. It is also used to contain an offset to address the location of a destination operand during string operations.

Segment registers

The memory areas allocated to program code, data and the machine stack are addressed separately, although these areas may overlap. At any given time there are four blocks of addressable memory available, termed *segments*, each of which may be up to 64K in length. (See Figure 1.)

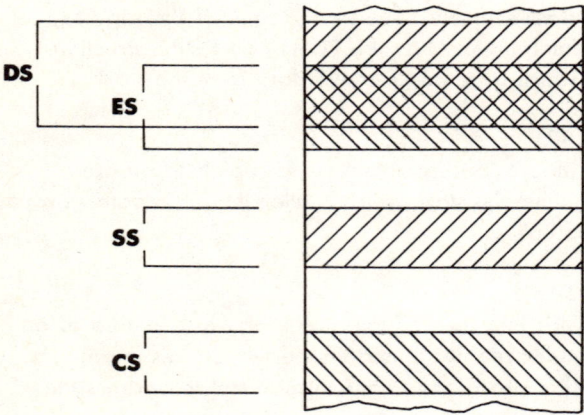

Figure 1 Example of segment allocation

The segment registers, CS, DS, SS and ES, are used to point to the base of the four addressable segments of memory: the *code* segment, the *data* segment, the *stack* segment and the *extra* segment; the 'extra' segment being an all-purpose data area.

The method by which a program instruction specifies the effective address of an operand within a segment is identical in both real and protected modes, although the system uses different methods of obtaining the base address of a segment in each mode.

In real address mode the actual base address of a segment is loaded into an appropriate segment register, while in protected mode a segment register is loaded with a *selector* value, which is used to obtain the full segment specification from a table stored elsewhere in memory. For application programming purposes, the segment base address and the selector may be regarded as being identical, since the segment specification in protected mode is handled automatically by the system.

Real mode address specification
A particular memory location within a segment is addressed by means of adding an offset value to the appropriate segment register. For example, the address of the next program instruction to be executed would be obtained by adding the value of the instruction pointer (IP) to the value of the code segment register, (CS). However, a memory location requires to be addressed by a 20-bit address value, whereas both CS and IP contain only 16-bit values. The full address is therefore obtained by shifting the contents of the CS register 4 bits to the left and resetting bits 0 to 3 (equivalent to multiplying CS by 16) and then adding the 16-bit value contained in IP.

In the following example, the code segment register contains the hex value D020 which, multiplied by 16, gives a code segment base value of D0200. The 16-bit offset in the IP register is ABCD which, when added to D0200, gives the address of the required memory location, which is DADCD.

The figures are given in both hexadecimal and decimal:

	Hex	Decimal
Value of CS register	D020	53280
CS times 16	D0200	852480
Value of IP register	ABCD	43981
Added to CS	= DADCD	896461

Locations within the other three segments are calculated in a similar manner, the segment and offset register combinations depending on the types of operations being performed.

By default, an operand address is assumed to be in the data segment and the segment register is therefore DS, with the offset contained in BX (the base data register), SI (the source index register) or DI (the destination index register).

If an offset is contained in a pointer register, such as SP or BP, the operand will be assumed to be contained in the stack segment and therefore the stack segment register (SS) will be used as the base. If the operand address is the destination of a string instruction, the extra segment register (ES) forms the base and the destination offset will be contained in DI. The source offset will be contained in SI.

In cases where the default registers are not required, the appropriate segment registers may be specified by a single byte instruction prefix.

Protected mode address specification
In protected mode, the use of offsets to specify particular memory locations is identical. However, the implementation of a protected, multi-user, multi-tasking environment within a larger address space requires a more complex system of allocating segment space and for verifying access to segments. The mechanism is entirely automatic and operates as follows.

Instead of loading a segment register with a real 16-bit base address specification, the program loads it with a 16-bit selector value. No special instructions or syntax are required for this operation and the assembly source code would be the same as that which would be used for real mode operation.

A *descriptor table register,* which is loaded by the OS and CPU, is used to identify the base address and the upper limit of a descriptor table, containing an array of data used for the interpretation of virtual address information for a specific range of data. The descriptor tables include the GDT (*Global Descriptor Table*), which contains descriptors for shared code and data resources, the IDT (*Interrupt Descriptor Table*), which contains descriptors for up to 256 interrupt service routines, and a number of LDTs (*Local Descriptor Tables*), which contain descriptors which are local to particular tasks.

A particular descriptor within a table is located by adding the selector code from the chosen segment register to the base of the descriptor table register and the data located at this address is then loaded into a *descriptor cache*, which is a hidden 48-bit extension to a segment register.

The descriptor cache contains three fields: the access rights field (8 bits), which indicates the type of segment to which the descriptor information refers (e.g. code or data segment); whether or not it is currently in physical memory; its access privilege level; whether it can be written to and/or read from; whether it is executable code and whether or not it has been accessed since being loaded into memory.

The segment size field of the cache (16 bits) indicates the total size of the segment, and the segment base address field (24 bits) contains the real base address of the segment. Note that this is 4 bits longer than the 20-bit base address used in real mode.

Finally, the offset specified within the instruction is added to the base address of the segment to give the effective address of the required operand.

IP (Instruction Pointer)

The instruction pointer is used to locate the position within the current code segment of the next instruction to be executed. Since the CS register contains the base address of the current code segment, then a particular 20-bit address within the segment is located by using IP as an offset from CS. In the following example, 'n' represents 1 bit:

```
  nnnnnnnnnnnnnnnn0000  CS contents plus 4 zeros
+         nnnnnnnnnnnnnnnn  IP contents
=   nnnnnnnnnnnnnnnnnnnn  Instruction address
```

In protected mode, the IP functions in exactly the same way except that it is added to the 24-bit segment base value contained in the code segment descriptor cache.

Flags register

The flags register is a 2-byte register containing twelve 'bit' flags which are used to indicate various conditions during the execution of a program. Bits 0, 2, 4, 6, 7 and 11 contain status flags which denote the results of program operations; bits 8 to 10 and 12 to 14 contain control flags; and bits 1, 3, 5 and 15 are not used.

15	14	13	12	11	10	9	8	7	6	5	4	3	2	1	0
	NT	IO	PL	OF	DF	IF	TF	SF	ZF		AF		PF		CF

The status flags may be tested after certain operations have been performed and the results used for conditional branching decisions. Their operations are as follows.

Carry flag (CF): bit 0 of the flags register
The carry flag is 'set' to 1 if an addition operation results in a 'carry', or if a subtraction operation results in a 'borrow'. If no carry is caused by an operation, then the carry flag is 'reset' to zero. The CF flag may also be reset using the CLC instruction and set using STC.

Parity flag (PF): bit 2 of the flags register
The parity flag is set when a value contains an even number of set bits and reset when a value contains an odd number of set bits.

Auxiliary carry flag (AF): bit 4 of the flags register
This operates in a similar way to the carry flag but is used to indicate a carry or borrow in the four low-order bits of BCD values.

Zero flag (ZF): bit 6 of the flags register
The zero flag is set when the result of an operation is zero. This may happen, for example, after a subtraction or decrementation instruction has been used or when a comparison has been made between two numbers of equal value. For results which are other than zero, the zero flag will be reset.

Sign flag (SF): bit 7 of the flags register
The sign flag is used to indicate whether a number is positive or negative in terms of two's complement arithmetic. The most significant bit of any value in two's complement is used to indicate a positive (reset) or negative (set) value and it is this bit which is copied into bit 7 of the flags register.

Overflow flag (OF): bit 11 of the flags register
Any result exceeding an operand's size limits will result in an overflow and will cause the overflow flag to be set.

Control flags

Trap flag (TF): bit 8 of the flags register
This bit is set to indicate that trap mode is in operation, causing the processor to single step through each instruction.

Interrupt flag (IF): bit 9 of the flags register
This is either reset to disable external interrupts or set to enable them. The IF flag is controlled by the STI and CLI instructions.

Direction flag (DF): bit 10 of the flags register
The direction flag is used to indicate the direction in which string instructions are being processed in relation to the SI and DI registers. It is reset for strings which are being processed in the direction of higher memory and set for strings which are being processed towards lower memory. The DF flag is controlled by the CLD and STD instructions.

IOPL and NT: bits 12—14 of the flags register
Two additional flags are located in the flags
register: IOPL (bits 12—13) and NT (bit 14). The
IOPL (I/O privilege level) field contains a 2-bit code
indicting the privilege level of I/O operations and is
used in conjunction with the privilege level
associated with a specific task as part of the
protection mechanism, to determine the right of the
task to execute privileged instructions.

The NT (nested task) flag is used by the system in
conjunction with the IRET instruction. When it is
reset, IRET will cause a return from interrupt to the
current task. When it is set, an IRET instruction will
cause a task switch to the previous task. These flags
are associated with multi-user, multi-tasking
operations and are not altered by applications
programs.

MSW (Machine Status Word)

The machine status word contains four bit flags. The
first, the PE (Protection Enable) flag is used to
indicate the current operating mode of the 80286.
On power-up or after a system reset, the PE flag is
reset, indicating real address mode, and when it is
set, using the LMSW instruction, the protected mode
is selected.

The remaining three flags in the MSW register
are used in connection with processor extensions. In
real address mode they have no significance, while
in protected mode they control the way in which
the processor responds to the presence or absence
of a co-processor extension when ESC and WAIT
instructions are used.

Task Register (TR)

The task register operates in a similar way to a segment descriptor and is used to locate a task state segment descriptor.

A unique task state descriptor is provided for every individual task and is used to specify its current parameters, including the values of all its segment, data, pointer and index registers plus links to any previous task.

When the task register is given a new selector value, for example when an inter-task call, jump or interrupt is requested, the parameters of the old task are preserved and those of the new task are copied from memory into a task state descriptor cache. Execution then commences with the new task.

Local Descriptor Table Register (LDTR)

Local Descriptor Tables (LDTs) are available to every task and are used to define all the descriptor information currently relating to them. The LDTR contains a selector which is used to address the descriptor data for a given task, which is then loaded into a cache by a mechanism similar to that used in the case of the segment registers. This information is used in conjunction with the GDT to determine the accessibility of a particular segment to a given task.

Global Descriptor Table Register (GDTR)

This register is similar in operation to the LDTR, except that it is used to address a Global Descriptor Table (GDT). Global descriptors are available to all tasks and are used to define those portions of memory, such as the operating system and shared data, which are accessible to all tasks. If a segment descriptor does not exist in the GDT or in the relevant LDT, a task is unable to address the segment.

Interrupt Descriptor Table Register (IDTR)

This register is used to address the interrupt descriptor table (IDT) which contains pointers to up to 256 interrupt service routines.

Memory Organization

Address organization in memory

Operands in memory locations may be stored or accessed in byte (8-bit) or word (16-bit) lengths as specified by the particular instructions used. Both byte and word length references may address either even- or odd-numbered memory locations.

Where word length data is being stored in memory, the byte containing the most significant bits of the word is stored at the higher memory address while the byte with the least significant bits is stored at the lower address.

For example, the value AABB, stored at address A25E, would be located as follows:

Address	Byte	
A25E	BB	Least significant byte
A25F	AA	Most significant byte

The 80286 accesses data in word lengths and where only 1 byte of data is required, the superfluous byte is discarded:

Byte access at even address (0000)

Address	Byte	
0000	AA	Byte accessed at address 0000
0001	nn	Following byte read and discarded

Word access at even address (0000)

Address	Byte	
0000	BB	Low-order byte at address 0000
0001	AA	High-order byte at address 0001

Where the address of the byte or word being addressed is odd, the procedure is somewhat different:

Byte access at odd address (0001)

Address	Byte	
0000	nn	Previous even byte read and discarded
0001	AA	Byte at specified odd address accessed

Word access at odd address (0001)

Address	Byte	
0000	nn	Previous even byte read and discarded
0001	BB	Low-order byte at specified odd address accessed
0002	AA	High-order byte accessed
0003	nn	Next odd byte read and discarded

Intel 80286 Instructions

Assembler syntax

It is usual to use an assembler program for encoding programs, rather than calculating the object code for each instruction individually.

An assembler accepts assembly language mnemonics and compiles them into object code automatically. For example, the instruction mnemonic **ADD AX,BX** means 'add the contents of register BX to register AX and let AX hold the result'. If this instruction were to be entered into an assembler program, it would be converted into its numeric form automatically, ready for execution.

An assembly language instruction consists of a mnemonic indicating the type of operation to be performed, such as DIV (divide) or SUB (subtract), and, in most cases, a suffix specifying the operand or operands affected by the instruction. The operands may be decimal, hexadecimal or binary constants; register operands, consisting of the contents of one or two byte registers, or memory operands, which may be addressed directly by means of user-defined labels representing fixed addresses, or indirectly addressed via the contents of registers. In the latter case, memory operands may be specified by combinations of offset values, such as constants, base registers and index registers. The following examples illustrate various forms of the ADD instruction:

ADD AX,100: add the immediate value 100 to register AX.

ADD ADDR,CL: add the contents of CL to the contents of the memory address corresponding to the value of the label 'ADDR'.

ADD AX,BX: add the contents of register BX to register AX.

ADD AX,[BX + DISP]: add to the AX register the contents of the memory location addressed by the sum of the contents of BX plus the value of the label 'DISP'.

The exact form of each mnemonic may vary among assemblers but will always follow a similar type of format, referred to as the assembler syntax. In this Handbook, all instructions are expressed in this type of format although in many cases a generic version of the syntax is used. For example, the above instructions were derived from the general syntactic form:

ADD destination,source

which means add a source operand to a destination operand. In many cases an instruction will specify only a source or a destination and in others there may be no operand specified, or it may be of an explicit type. For example, HLT (halt) does not require an operand and IN (input) specifically requires a port specification.

The generic syntax for each instruction, indicating the types of operands required, is given in the Glossary starting on page 53. A list of permissible addressing modes is also given, indicating the means by which operands may be specified: whether, for example, the source and/or destination operands consist of immediate data or whether they are located in registers or in memory addresses.

Since the addresses of all memory operands are within a particular segment, the value of the appropriate segment register is taken into account although normally it is not explicitly incorporated in the instruction. For example, the instruction **ADD AX,ADDR** adds the contents of the memory address specified by the value of 'ADDR' to AX. The memory address is assumed by default to be in the data segment of memory and therefore 'ADDR' is not an absolute address but an offset which is added automatically to the value of the data segment (DS) register. If some other segment is required, then it needs to be stated explicitly by means of a prefix, e.g. **ADD AX,ES:ADDR** where the data will be in the extra segment.

The various permissible combinations of registers, constants and labels which may be used to address operands are termed addressing modes and the following section describes the various modes available, together with diagrams illustrating the ways in which the operand addresses are calculated.

Although various examples of mnemonic instructions are given, the precise format of assembly language commands will tend to vary between assemblers. In some cases, for example, the instruction **MOV DX,[BX + DI]** might be expressed as **MOV DX,[BX][DI]** or **MOV AX,[BX + DISP]** as **MOV AX,DISP[BX]** and readers should therefore refer to the appropriate assembler documentation.

Addressing Modes

The addressing modes employed by the 80286 are register, immediate, direct, indirect, indirect with base, indirect with index and indirect with base and index. These operate as follows:

Immediate addressing

The operand is a constant which immediately follows the instruction code. For example, the instruction **MOV BL,8A** moves the constant value 8A into register BL.

MOV BL,8A | Reg. BL | ←——— 8A

Examples: **ADD AL,8   MOV BX,365 CMP AL,56   AND CX,66   TEST CX,40**

Register addressing

The operands in this case are the contents of specified registers and, in the case of general data registers, may be of either byte or word length. For example, **MOV AH,BL** moves the byte value contained in register BL into register AH. The instruction **MOV AX,BX** moves the word value contained in register BX into register AX.

MOV AX,BX

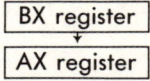

Examples: **MOV CX,DX   ADD AL,DL CMP AX,DX**

Direct (or absolute) addressing

The operand is located at an address specified in the instruction. For example, the instruction **MOV AX,ADDR** moves the value in the address pointed to by the label 'ADDR' into register AX. 'ADDR' is a constant which forms an offset which is added to the value of the base register of the segment in which the required address is located (times 16), as follows:

MOV AX,ADDR

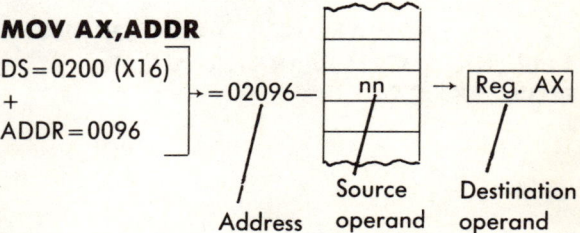

29

The segment register is assumed by default to be the current data segment register (DS). However, any of the other segments may be selected by specifying the required segment register within the instruction. For example, the extra segment is specified in the instruction **MOV AX,ES:ADDR**

Examples: **ADD NUMSTORE,6**
AND ADDR1,1   CMP AL,NUMSTORE
INC ADDR2   MOV BX,ASTORE
MOV ADDR1,BX   ROL NUM,CL

Indirect addressing

The operand is located at an address pointed to by either a base or index register such as BX, BP, SI or DI. For example, in the instruction **MOV CX,[DI]** the source operand is located at an address computed by the addition of the contents of the DI register to the contents of the appropriate segment register (times 16) which in this case would be DS:

MOV CX,[DI]

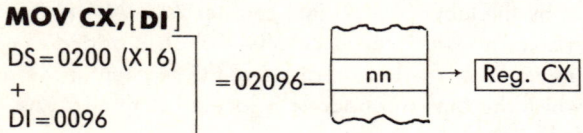

$$DS = 0200 \ (X16)$$
$$+$$
$$DI = 0096$$

$= 02096 -$ nn $\rightarrow$ Reg. CX

Examples: **ADD AX,[BX]   AND [BX],AX**
CMP [BX],DX   IDIV [BX],ANUMBR
MOV [BX],CX

Register indirect with base

The operand is located at an address specified by the addition of a segment register (times 16), a 16-bit internal register (BX or BP) and an 8- or 16-bit displacement. For example, **MOV AX,[BX + DISP]** moves the contents of the address pointed to by the current segment register + DISP + BX into AX:

MOV AX,[BX + DISP]

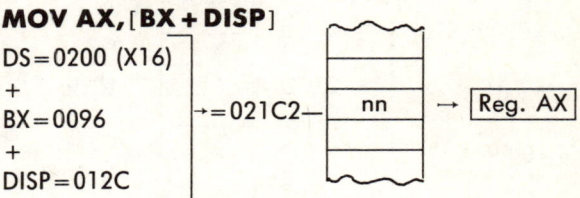

DS = 0200 (X16)
+
BX = 0096
+
DISP = 012C

→ = 021C2 — nn → [Reg. AX]

Examples: **ADD AX,[BX + DISP]**
AND [BX + DISP],CX   CMP [BX + DISP],80
DEC [BP + DISP]   CMP [BX + 8],SI

Register indirect with index

The operand is located at an address specified by the addition of a segment register, an index register (SI or DI) and an 8- or 16-bit displacement. For example, **MOV AX, [DI + DISP]** moves the contents of the address pointed to by the current segment register (times 16) + DI + DISP into AX:

MOV AX, [DI + DISP]

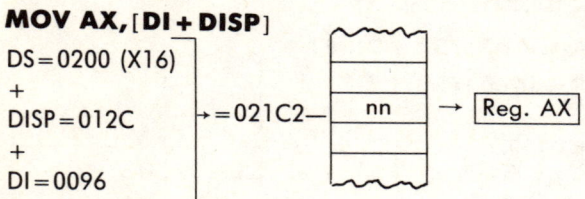

DS = 0200 (X16)
+
DISP = 012C
+
DI = 0096

= 021C2 — nn → Reg. AX

Examples: **ADD AX, [DI + DISP]**
AND [DI + DISP],CX   CMP [SI + DISP],20
DEC [DI + DISP]   CMP [SI + 8],DI

32

Register indirect with base and index

The operand is located at an address specified by the addition of a segment register, two internal registers and an optional 8- or 16-bit displacement. For example, **MOV AX, [BX + DI + DISP]** moves the contents of the address pointed to by the current segment register (times 16) + BX + DI + DISP into AX:

MOV AX, [BX + DI + DISP]

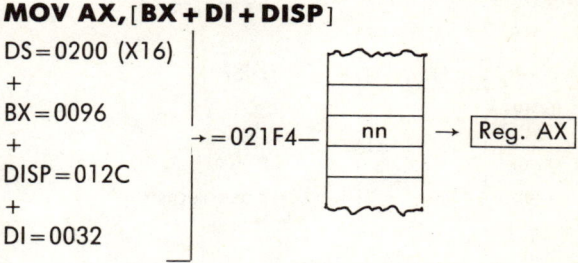

DS = 0200 (X16)
+
BX = 0096
+
DISP = 012C
+
DI = 0032

→ = 021F4 — nn → Reg. AX

Examples: **ADD [BX + DI + DISP] , AX**
MOV [BX + DI] , AX
CMP AX, [BX + DI + DISP]   DEC [BP + SI]
AND AL, [BX + DI + DISP]

The memory addressing modes provide a particularly flexible means of accessing data. However, the combinations of registers and displacements and the ways in which they relate to actual data structures in memory may not always be clear. The three types of indirect addressing, based addressing, indexed addressing and based indexed addressing, are suitable for addressing different types of data structures, and the following examples should help to clarify these methods.

33

Based addressing

In based addressing, the base address of the block of memory being accessed is stored in one of two registers: BX or BP. If the memory block is within the stack segment, then BP is used. The effective address within the appropriate segment is computed from the base register plus an 8- or 16-bit displacement. For example, in the following array the required data is referenced by BX+DISP:

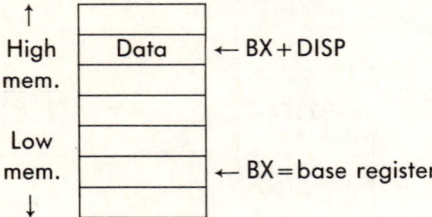

Indexed addressing

In indexed addressing the SI and DI registers are used. In this case, however, it is the displacement value which forms the base of the memory block and the register forms an index offset. In the following array the required data is referenced by DI+ARRAYSTART:

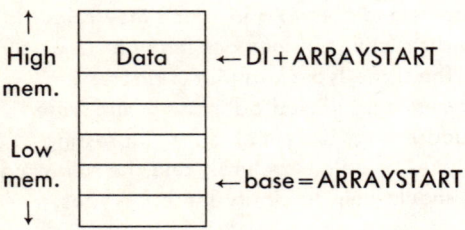

Based indexed addressing

In based indexed addressing the required address is referenced by a base register (BX or BP) plus an index register (SI or DI) plus an optional displacement value. By this means, a block of individual records may be referenced by two variables. For example, a block of memory may hold a series of records indicating, say, monthly sales figures, with one variable pointing to the required year and one to the required month. In the following example, month 7 is addressed by BX + DI:

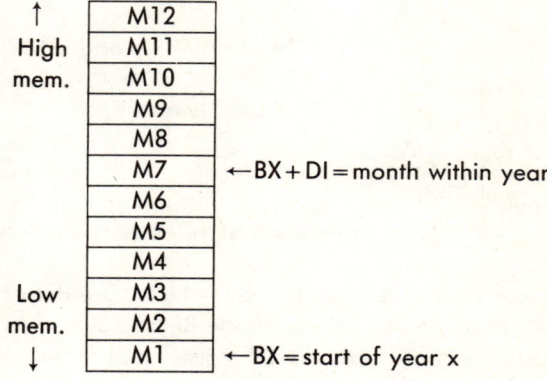

```
  ↑      ┌──────┐
High     │ M12  │
mem.     │ M11  │
         │ M10  │
         │  M9  │
         │  M8  │
         │  M7  │ ←BX + DI = month within year
         │  M6  │
         │  M5  │
         │  M4  │
Low      │  M3  │
mem.     │  M2  │
  ↓      │  M1  │ ←BX = start of year x
         └──────┘
```

However, with complex arrangements of information it would be more useful to be able to reference not only an item within a block but an item within a block containing several arrays. For example, a block of memory may hold a series of records indicating, say, quarterly sales figures for a three-year period. In the following example, quarter 3 of year 2 is addressed by BX + DI + DISP:

↑	Q4
High	Q3
mem.	Q2
	Q1
	Q4
	Q3	← BX + DI + DISP (quarter 3)
	Q2
	Q1	← BX + DISP (year 2)
	Q4
Low	Q3
mem.	Q2
↓	Q1	← BX = base of block (year 1)

In cases where the body of the stack contains data which needs to be referenced, the BP and SI registers may be used. The BP register (not to be confused with SS, the stack segment register) points to the base of the required data area and the SI (source index) register is used as an offset, together with a displacement constant if required.

For all indirect modes, pre-defined segment and offset register values can be stored as data and loaded into the appropriate registers when needed. This procedure is described in the Glossary under the instruction headings LEA, LDS and LES.

To summarize, a memory operand may be addressed by any combination of an 8- or 16-bit displacement, a base register and an index register, as follows:

Direct:	displacement
Indirect:	BX, BP, SI or DI
Based:	BX or BP with 8- or 16-bit disp.
Indexed:	SI or DI with 8- or 16-bit disp.
Based indexed:	BX or BP with DI or SI and with optional 8- or 16-bit disp.

Note that 8-bit displacements are sign-extended to 16 bits and that any carry resulting from the addition of 16-bit values is ignored.

Instruction Object Codes

Instruction object codes are between 1 and 6 bytes in length, according to the type of instruction and the addressing mode used. The formats appropriate to each instruction and its modes are indicated in the Instruction Glossary in the second half of this Handbook.

In general, instructions are encoded using three different types of codes: the instruction opcode, the effective address code, plus bytes or words containing displacement constants. For example:

| Opcode | D | W | MOD | REG | R/M | data low | data high |

The following is an example of the encoding format for an instruction to move a memory or register operand to or from a register operand:

| 100010 | D | W | MOD | REG | R/M |

The binary code 100010 constitutes the fixed opcode for this instruction and the letters in bit positions 0 and 1 of the first byte indicate the fields into which the remaining information is placed. Their functions are as follows:

D (1 bit)
The D (destination) bit field is reset if data is required to be returned in a destination specified by the 'MOD' and 'R/M' fields. It is set if the data is required to be returned in a destination specified by the 'REG' field.

W (1 bit)
The W (word or byte) bit field is reset if the operand is of byte length and set if it is of word length.

The second byte contains the effective address specification, using three fields which function as follows:

REG (3 bits)

The REG (register) field contains a code indicating a register, and the range of register codes used is listed in Table 1. In some instructions, this field is given a fixed value, which constitutes an extension to the opcode. In some other cases the REG field is located in the three low-order bits of the first byte of the instruction.

MOD (2 bits)

The MOD (mode) field is used to indicate whether the displacement section of an instruction code is zero, a sign-extended 8-bit datum or a word length datum. If the MOD field contains the code 11, then the operand is in a register rather than in memory and therefore the R/M field is treated as a REG field.

R/M (3 bits)

The R/M (register or memory) field specifies either a register (when MOD=11) or the base and index register and displacement combinations for referencing operands located in memory. Table 2 shows the various combinations. The suffix dExt represents a sign-extended 8-bit datum and dL and dH represent the low and high bytes of a word length datum respectively.

Table 1 *REG field codes*

Code	Word reg.	Byte reg.
	W = 1	W = 0
000	AX	AL
001	CX	CL
010	DX	DL
011	BX	BL
100	SP	AH
101	BP	CH
110	SI	DH
111	DI	BH

Other field symbols used in certain instructions are
S, V and Z and the meanings of these are indicated
on the 'Key to symbols and abbreviations' page at
the beginning of the Instruction Glossary.

Table 2 *MOD and R/M field codes*

R/M	MOD: 00	01	10	11 (W = 0)	11 (W = 1)
000	BX + SI	BX + SI + dExt	BX + SI + dL/dH	REG: AL	AX
001	BX + DI	BX + DI + dExt	BX + DI + dL/dH	REG: CL	CX
010	BP + SI	BP + SI + dExt	BP + SI + dL/dH	REG: DL	DX
011	BP + DI	BP + DI + dExt	BP + DI + dL/dH	REG: BL	BX
100	SI	SI + dExt	SI + dL/dH	REG: AH	SP
101	DI	DI + dExt	DI + dL/dH	REG: CH	BP
110	dL/dH	BP + dExt	BP + dL/dH	REG: DH	SI
111	BX	BX + dExt	BX + dL/dH	REG: BH	DI

The following examples illustrate three typical object code formats, showing how the coding in the various fields relates to some of the addressing modes listed in the previous section:

Example 1

Op.	REG
01001	011

This example corresponds to the instruction **DEC BX** which decrements the BX register. 01001 is the fixed opcode for this operation and the register specification, which is entered in the REG field, is obtained from Table 1.

Example 2

Opcode	W	MOD	Op.	R/M
1111111	0	00	001	001

Example 2 corresponds to the instruction **DEC [BX + DI]** which decrements the data stored at the address pointed to by the BX and DI registers.

In this case the opcode for DEC is split between the first and second bytes of the instruction and specifies that the operand is to be found in memory rather than in a register. The W bit is reset, indicating a byte-sized operand. The MOD field contains the code 00 and R/M contains 001 which, referring to Table 2, specifies an operand location pointed to by BX + DI. The address of the operand is calculated as follows:

Segment register + 0000
+	Base reg. (BX)
+	Index reg. (DI)
=	20-bit operand address

Example 3

Opcode	D	W	MOD	REG	R/M	Disp lo	Disp hi
100010	1	1	10	001	001	11110100	00000001

Example 3 corresponds to the instruction **MOV CX,** [**BX + DI + 500**] which moves the contents of the memory address pointed to by BX + DI + 500 into register CX. In this case the D bit is set, indicating that the data destination is the register specified in the REG field: in this case, CX. The W bit is set, indicating that the operand is of word length. The MOD and R/M fields contain the codes 10 and 001 respectively, indicating that the offset for the required source operand is obtained from BX + DI plus the 16-bit displacement constant contained in the following two bytes. The address of the operand is calculated as follows:

Segment register + 0000
+	16-bit disp. (500)
+	Base reg. (BX)
+	Index reg. (DI)
=	20-bit operand address

Where the default segment register needs to be overridden, a segment override prefix is used, which takes the form:

| 001 | SEG | 110 |

The SEG section is used to hold the codes 00, 01, 10 or 11, representing the current extra, code, stack and data segments respectively.

Stack Operations

The stack segment is a block of memory addressed by means of offsets to the SS (stack segment) register. Individual locations within the stack are addressed by adding an offset contained in the stack pointer register (SP) to the contents of SS.

Data is stored on the stack in word lengths, by means of the PUSH instruction, which decrements SP by two and places the data at the corresponding stack address. Removal of data from the stack is achieved using the POP instruction which copies data from the top of the stack into a destination register and then increments the SP register by two. Note that the stack extends downwards in memory and data is stored and retrieved on a LIFO (last in, first out) basis.

Dynamic storage areas allocated within a stack are referenced by means of the BP (Base Pointer) register.

Interrupts

Interrupts may be initiated by external devices, by internal conditions or by software.

External interrupts are signalled via the INTR (interrupt) and NMI (non-maskable interrupt) pins. The INTR pin may be enabled or disabled by setting the IF (enable interrupt flag) in the flags register to either 1 or 0 respectively, using the instructions STI (set interrupt enable) or CLI (clear interrupt enable). Non-maskable interrupts cannot, by definition, be disabled and are given priority over maskable interrupts.

When a maskable interrupt occurs, the operation which is currently being executed is first completed, following which the current environment, represented by the contents of the flags register, the CS register and the IP register, is saved on the stack for retrieval when the interrupt has been serviced.

The interrupting device then supplies an 8-bit interrupt 'type' code, indicating the type of interrupt which is taking place, and this code is used to reference a look-up table of interrupt vector addresses (the IDT) which point to the locations of up to 256 interrupt handling routines. Two addresses are copied from the table, one being the base address of the segment in which the required interrupt handling routine is located, which is copied into CS, and the other being the required offset within the segment, which is copied into IP. CS and IP together give the start address of the relevant interrupt handling routine and execution commences from that address.

When the interrupt has been serviced, the previous environment is retrieved from the stack and normal program execution commences from the address of the instruction following that which was being executed prior to the interrupt.

Internal interrupts are initiated by conditions which would interfere with the flow of execution such as attempts to divide by zero, the use of an invalid opcode or attempts to communicate with a non-existent extension processor. These interrupts are classified as 'exceptions' and their interrupt type codes are generated internally.

Software interrupts are controlled by the INT (interrupt) and INTO (interrupt on overflow) instructions, with a return from the interrupt service routine being signalled by the IRET instruction.

There may be up to 256 interrupt handling routines in a system, the first 32 of which are reserved and the remainder of which are applicable to particular system configurations. The following table gives a summary of the interrupt types and their type codes.

Table 3 *Interrupt types*

Division by zero	0
Single stepping trap	1
NMI interrupt	2
Breakpoint	3
Overflow on INTO	4
BOUND range exceeded	5
Invalid opcode	6
Extension not present	7
Double fault exception	8
Processor extension segment overrun	9
Invalid task state segment	10
Segment not present	11
Stack segment overrun or not present	12
General protection exception	13
Reserved	14 – 15
Extension error	16
Reserved	17 – 31
User vectors	32 – 255

The interrupt table occupies addresses 0000 to 03FF. When protected mode is initialized, the LIDT instruction is used to set a 24-bit base address for the interrupt table, together with a 16-bit limit. The interrupt types remain the same as those in real mode, although some of the exceptions are applicable only to protected mode operation.

I/O

In the 80286 the I/O address space is separate
from memory and utilizes separate control lines.
Only the most significant 16 bits of an I/O address
are used to specify an I/O port and the range is
therefore limited to 64K byte or 32K word ports.
Port addresses F8 to FF are reserved and may not
therefore be used for system applications.

Since both I/O and memory share the same
address bus, the distinction between memory
read/write and I/O read/write operations is
determined by which of the two control lines is
currently active.

Data may be read from or written to a fixed
port, specified by a constant in the range 0 to 255,
or to a variable port specified by the contents of
the DX register, in which case the range is 0 to
65535. Data may be of byte length, in which case
it is moved to or from the AL register, or of word
length, in which case it is moved to or from the AX
register.

For data transferred to or from a port specified
by a constant, two bytes are required to specify the
operation. For IN operations the first byte is coded
as 1110010W, for OUT operations as 1110011W;
the W bit being set for word operands and reset
for byte operands. The second byte contains the
address of the required port. For example:

1110010000010110 = **IN AL,22** transfers a byte
from port 22 to AL
1110010100010110 = **IN AX,22** transfers a
word from port 22 to AX
11100110000010110 = **OUT 22,AL** transfers a
byte from AL to port 22
11100111100010110 = **OUT 22,AX** transfers a
word from AX to port 22

For data transfers to or from a port specified by the
contents of the DX register, only one byte is
required: 1110110W for IN operations and
1110111W for OUT operations, the W bit again
being set for word operands and reset for byte
operands. For example:

11101100 = **IN AL,DX**
11101101 = **IN AX,DX**
11101110 = **OUT DX,AL**
11101111 = **OUT DX,AX**

Two block I/O instructions, INS and OUTS, are
also provided, which enable the input and output of
byte or word strings between I/O ports and
memory. Like the other string instructions, these can
be prefixed by the REP (repeat) instruction and
reiterated. These instructions use DX to specify the
I/O port and CX to specify the iteration count.

In protected mode, a general exception is
initiated if a Task's CPL (current privilege level) is
greater than the IOPL (I/O privilege level) and also,
in the case of INS and OUTS, if the memory access
is beyond the segment limit or if access rights are
violated.

Protection

The protection facilities provided on the 80286 are
designed to prevent the operating system and data
from being corrupted by applications programs and
to prevent individual tasks from interfering with
each other.

Privilege
One of the primary protection mechanisms is the
system of privilege levels, governing the extent to
which any given task may access any other part of
the system. The highest level of privilege, level 0, is
given to the operating system kernel. Special service
routines and customized extensions to the operating
system will normally be allocated privilege levels 1
and 2, while applications programs operate at level
3, the least privileged level.

In general, the principle governing privileged
access rights is that tasks are permitted to access
data at a privilege level numerically equal to, or
greater than, their own. This arrangement means
that system data, which has a high privilege level, is
protected from interference by low privilege tasks
such as applications programs, although operating
system service routines may be included in the
global address space so that they can be called as
procedures by programs of a lower privilege level.

Note that as an additional protection feature, separate stacks are maintained at each privilege level, and data used in inter-level calls is automatically copied over from one stack to the other. Tasks may also have their own, private, local address space allocated for their own exclusive data. This is pointed to by a Local Descriptor Table (LDT).

Types
A further level of protection is achieved by means of the division of individual segments into four different types: execute only, execute and read, read only, and read and write. In operation, built-in checking mechanisms ensure that segment type parameters are not violated, either during the process of selector loading or when access to a segment is requested during the execution of an instruction. Thus it is impossible for the code segment register to be loaded with a data segment specification or for a program to attempt to read a code segment rather than execute it.

Instructions
To ensure that tasks with a lower privilege level have no means by which to alter the parameters of the system, those instructions which are used to set parameters are privileged. These will cause an error exception if they are used by a task with an insufficient privilege level, and they include LIDT, LLDT, LGDT, LTR, LMSW, CTS and HALT. Similarly, I/O instructions and those which alter the maskable interrupt flag are also given a privilege level (IOPL) and may therefore be restricted to privileged tasks.

These include IN, INS, OUT, OUTS, STI, CLI and LOCK. Certain instructions are only applicable to protected mode operation and will not be effective in real address mode. These are: LLDT, SLDT, LTR, STR, LAR, LSL VERR. Other protected mode instructions, such as CTS, LGDT, SGDT, LIDT, SIDT, LMSW and SMSW, may be used in real mode in order to initialize the system for protected mode operation.

Instruction restart
Certain instructions, such as those which load segments or which reference the stack, are automatically restartable after an exception has occurred. For example, an attempt to access a segment held in virtual memory will result in a 'segment not present' exception and, after the system has loaded the required segment into physical memory, the original instruction will be restarted. Likewise, in cases where multi-tasking operations threaten to cause a stack overflow, the processor intercepts any instruction which is likely to lead to this condition and initiates a corrective intercept, after which execution restarts and continues normally.

Pointers
A number of instructions are provided for checking access calls and ensuring that they do not pass incorrect pointers which might result in the subsequent corruption of data. These instructions are: ARPL, VERR, VERW, LSL and LAR.

Virtual Memory Management

In addition to the 16Mbyte real address space available in protected mode, a virtual store of up to one gigabyte (2^{30} bytes) may be accessed by each user. In normal circumstances, where a segment is resident in real address space, memory access is controlled by the information located in the appropriate segment descriptor cache. However, when an instruction requires access to a segment which is stored in virtual memory, which is indicated by a 'not present' bit in its descriptor, an exception is initiated.

The operating system reserves the required amount of free space for the virtual segment by swapping it with a segment which is currently resident in real memory. A segment usage mechanism, whereby an 'access' bit in the descriptor is updated every time a segment is accessed, ensures that a segment swapped out of memory to make way for a virtual segment will be one with a low level of usage recorded.

The segment descriptor is then updated and the new segment is marked as being 'present'. On completion of the exception, the original instruction is automatically re-started and access to the required segment is then handled by the normal procedures.

Instruction Set Glossary

Key to symbols and abbreviations

Syntax

source	source operand
dest	destination operand
routine__name	indicates procedure label
opcode	opcode for co-processor in ESC instruction
addr	operand address for ESC instruction
port	port number
dest__string	destination string label
source__string	source string label
counter__value	reiteration value (constant or CL or CX contents) for loops, shifts and rotations

Addressing modes

acc.	operand in accumulator: AX or AL
mem.	operand in memory
imm.	immediate operand
reg.	operand in register

Opcode fields

MOD	mode
REG	source or destination register
R/M	register or memory indicator
W	byte or word flag
D	indicates destination

S	indicates short instruction: If S=0, then operand = 16 bits of immediate data. If S=1 and W=1, the 8 bits of immediate data are sign extended to form the operand
V	If V=0, then the counter value = 1. If V=1, then the counter value is in CL
Z	loop repetition indicator: if Z=0, then loop while zero flag is reset, otherwise repeat while zero flag is set
DATA LO	low-order byte of immediate data
DATA HI	high-order byte of immediate data
DISP	low-order byte of displacement, sign-extended to 16 bits
DISP LO	low-order byte of displacement
DISP HI	high-order byte of displacement
LEVEL	lexical nesting level for ENTER
OFFSET LO	low byte of new IP value in call and jump instructions
OFFSET HI	high byte of new IP value in call and jump instructions
SEG LO	low byte of segment register in call and jump instructions
SEG HI	high byte of segment register in call and jump instructions
TYPE NO	represents type number for interrupts

Flags

A	altered by operation
0	reset
1	set
?	status undefined
X	not affected

AAA (ASCII adjust for addition)

Syntax: AAA
Modes and object code format:

00110111

Mnemonic	Operation	Flags: O D I T S Z A P C
AAA	ASCII adjust for addition	? ? ? A ? A

Description: AAA is used to convert the contents of the AL register to an unpacked binary-coded decimal number. If the four least significant bits of AL are greater than 9 or if the AF flag is set, then 6 is added to AL, 1 is added to AH, AF is set, CF is made equal to AF, and AL is ANDed with the constant 0F. The four most significant bits of AL are reset.

AAD (ASCII adjust for division)

Syntax: AAD
Modes and object code format:

11010101	00001010

Mnemonic	Operation	Flags: O D I T S Z A P C
AAD	ASCII adjust for division	? A A ? A ?

Description: AAD converts two unpacked binary-coded decimal numbers to a single byte dividend prior to a division operation. The original BCD values are held in the AH and AL registers and the number is returned in AL. AH is zeroed.

AAM (ASCII adjust for multiply)

Syntax: AAM
Modes and object code format:

11010100	00001010

Mnemonic	Operation	Flags: O D I T S Z A P C
AAM	ASCII adjust for multiply	? A A ? A ?

Description: AAM converts the binary product of
the unsigned multiplication of two unpacked BCD
values into BCD. Prior to multiplication, the
unpacked BCD values are stored in AH and AL with
their high order nibbles equal to zero. Following
multiplication, the product, in register AX, is
converted by AAM into two BCD bytes in registers
AH and AL.

AAS (ASCII adjust for subtraction)

Syntax: AAS
Modes and object code format:

00111111

Mnemonic	Operation	Flags: O D I T S Z A P C
AAS	ASCII adjust for subtraction	? ? ? A ? A

Description: AAS converts the result of the
subtraction of two unpacked BCD operands into an
unpacked decimal number. The result is held in the
AL register and bits 4 to 7 are zeroed.

ADC (add with carry)

Syntax: ADC dest,source
Modes and object code format:

Reg. or mem. with reg. to reg. or mem.:

000100DW	MOD REG R/M

Imm. to reg. or mem.:

100000SW	MOD 010 R/M	DATA	DATA IF S:W=01

Imm. to acc.:

0001010W	DATA	DATA IF W=1

Mnemonic	Operation	Flags: O D I T S Z A P C
ADC	Add with carry	A A A A A A

Description: The signed or unsigned source and destination operands are added together and, if the CF flag is set, the result is incremented by 1. The result is returned in the destination.

ADD (addition)

Syntax: ADD dest,source
Modes and object code format:

Reg. or mem. with reg. to reg. or mem.:

000000DW	MOD REG R/M

Imm. to reg. or mem.:

100000SW	MOD 000 R/M	DATA	DATA IF S:W=01

Imm. to acc.:

0000010W	DATA	DATA IF W=1

Mnemonic	Operation	Flags: O D I T S Z A P C
ADD	Addition	A A A A A A

Description: The source and destination operands are added together with the result being returned in the destination.

AND (AND logical)

Syntax: AND dest,source
Modes and object code format:

Reg. or mem. and reg. to reg. or mem.:

001000DW	MOD REG R/M

Imm. to reg. or mem.:

1000000W	MOD 100 R/M	DATA	DATA IF W=1

Imm. to acc.:

0010010W	DATA	DATA IF W=1

Mnemonic	Operation	Flags: O D I T S Z A P C
AND	AND logical	0 A A ? A 0

Description: AND is a logical operation which
ANDs a source operand with a destination operand
and stores the result in the destination. For each
corresponding bit in the source and destination
operands the result is a 1 if both bits are set,
otherwise zero.

ARPL (adjust requested privilege level)

Syntax: ARPL source
Modes and object code format:

01100011	MOD REG R/M

Mnemonic	Operation	Flags: O D I T S Z A P C
ARPL	Adjust requested priv. level	A

Description: ARPL is a pointer testing instruction
which is used to check that a selector value does
not violate a set privilege level. It adjusts the
requested privilege level (RPL) of the selector to the
numeric maximum of its original value and the RPL
in the register. If the RPL is altered by this
instruction the ZF flag is set.

BOUND (array bounds check)

Syntax: BOUND dest,source
Modes and object code format:

01100010	MOD REG R/M

Mnemonic	Operation	Flags: O D I T S Z A P C
BOUND	Detect value out of range	

Description: BOUND specifies a register containing
an index offset for an array. If the offset is beyond
the specified boundary limit for the array, a
corrective exception may be invoked. This enables
arrays to be checked for length before read or
write operations are attempted.

CALL (call subroutine)

Syntax: CALL routine__name
Modes and object code format:

Intra-segment direct:

11101000	DISP LO	DISP HI

Intra-segment indirect:

11111111	MOD 010 R/M

Inter-segment direct:

10011010	OFFSET LO	OFFSET HI
	SEG LO	SEG HI

Inter-segment indirect:

11111111	MOD 011 R/M

Mnemonic	Operation	Flags: O D I T S Z A P C
CALL	Call subroutine	

Description: CALL is used to direct execution to the address of a specified subroutine. Calls may be direct or indirect and may either reference subroutines within the same segment (intra-segment calls) or in other segments (inter-segment calls). The operations of each type of call are as follows:

Direct intra-segment call: the IP register is pushed on to the stack and the target address is calculated as IP plus a signed 16-bit displacement.

Direct inter-segment call: the CS register is pushed on to the stack and replaced by a 16-bit segment value. The IP register is then pushed on to the stack and replaced by a 16-bit offset value.

Indirect intra-segment call: the IP register is pushed on to the stack and the target location is calculated as IP plus either a memory word or the value of a 16-bit general register.

Indirect inter-segment call: the CS and IP registers are pushed on to the stack and replaced by the two words located at the memory address specified by the effective address field.

CBW (convert byte to word)

Syntax: CBW
Modes and object code format:

```
10011000
```

Mnemonic	Operation	Flags: O D I T S Z A P C
CBW	Convert byte to word	

Description: CBW is used to sign extend the byte contained in register AL to a word value by copying the value of the most significant bit of AL into each of the bits in AH.

CLC (clear carry)

Syntax: CLC
Modes and object code format:

```
11111000
```

Mnemonic	Operation	Flags: O D I T S Z A P C
CLC	Clear carry flag	X X X X X 0

Description: CLC is used to reset the carry flag.

62

CLD (clear direction flag)

Syntax: CLD
Modes and object code format:

11111100

Mnemonic	Operation	Flags: O D I T S Z A P C
CLD	Clear direction flag	0 X X

Description: CLD resets the DF flag. The effect of the operation is to cause the SI and/or the DI registers to be autoincremented during subsequent string instructions. Note that when DF is set, the registers are autodecremented.

CLI (clear interrupt enable)

Syntax: CLI
Modes and object code format:

11111010

Mnemonic	Operation	Flags: O D I T S Z A P C
CLI	Clear interrupt enable flag	X 0 X

Description: CLI disables maskable interrupts by resetting the IF flag.

CMC (complement carry flag)

Syntax: CMC
Modes and object code format:

```
11110101
```

Mnemonic	Operation	Flags: O D I T S Z A P C
CMC	Complement carry flag	X X X X X A

Description: CMC sets the CF flag if it is reset or resets it if it is set.

CMP (compare)

Syntax: CMP dest,source
Modes and object code format:

Reg. or mem. and reg.:

001110DW	MOD REG R/M

Imm. with reg. or mem.:

100000SW	MOD 111 R/M	DATA	DATA IF S:W=01

Imm. with acc.:

0011110W	DATA	DATA IF W=1

Mnemonic	Operation	Flags: O D I T S Z A P C
CMP	Comparison	A A A A A A

Description: CMP subtracts a source from a destination operand without storing the result and without affecting the original value of either. The flags are affected by the operation, permitting subsequent conditional branching operations.

CMPS (compare string)

Syntax: CMPS
Modes and object code format:

1010011W

Mnemonic	Operation	Flags: O D I T S Z A P C
CMPS	String comparison	A A A A A A

Description: CMPS compares two strings by subtracting the destination from the source. Neither of the operands are altered, but the flags are affected and may be tested accordingly. The source string is addressed by the SI register and the destination by DI, and both registers are either autoincremented or autodecremented after the comparison, depending on the status of the DF flag. *See also* REPE, REPZ, REPNE and REPNZ.

CTS (clear task switched flag)

Syntax: CTS
Modes and object code format:

00001111	00000110

Mnemonic	Operation	Flags: O D I T S Z A P C
CTS	Clear task switched flag	

Description: CTS is a privileged instruction which clears the task switched (TS) flag.

CWD (convert word)

Syntax: CWD
Modes and object code format:

10011001

Mnemonic	Operation	Flags: O D I T S Z A P C
CWD	Convert word to long word	

Description: CWD is used to sign extend the word value contained in register AX to a 32-bit value by copying the value of the most significant bit of AX into each of the bits in DX.

DAA (decimal adjust for addition)

Syntax: DAA
Modes and object code format:

00100111

Mnemonic	Operation	Flags: O D I T S Z A P C
DAA	Decimal adjust for addition	? A A A A A

Description: DAA is used to convert the contents of the AL register into a pair of packed binary-coded decimal values after addition operations. If the four least significant bits of AL are greater than 9 or if the AF flag is set, then AL is incremented by 6 and the AF flag is set. If the high-order bits of AL are greater than 9 or if the CF flag is set, then AL is incremented by the hex value 60 and CF is set.

DAS (decimal adjust for subtraction)

Syntax: DAS
Modes and object code format:

00101111

Mnemonic	Operation	Flags: O D I T S Z A P C
DAS	Decimal adjust for subtract	? A A A A A

Description: DAS is used to convert the contents of
the AL register into a pair of packed binary-coded
decimal values after subtraction operations. If the
four least significant bits of AL are greater than 9
or if the AF flag is set, then AL is decremented by 6
and the AF flag is set. If the high-order bits of AL
are greater than 9 or if the CF flag is set, then AL
is decremented by 60 and CF is set.

DEC (decrement)

Syntax: DEC dest
Modes and object code format:

Reg. or mem.:

1111111W	MOD 001 R/M

Reg:

01001REG

Mnemonic	Operation	Flags: O D I T S Z A P C
DEC	Decrementation	A A A A A X

Description: DEC decrements the value of the
destination operand by 1.

DIV (divide)

Syntax: DIV source
Modes and object code format:

1111011W	MOD 110 R/M

Mnemonic	Operation	Flags:	O	D	I	T	S	Z	A	P	C
DIV	Unsigned division		?				?	?	?	?	?

Description: DIV is used to divide the unsigned contents of the accumulator by a source operand. Where the source operand is of byte length, the dividend is originally stored in registers AL and AH, and after the division operation the integer quotient and remainder are returned in AL and AH respectively. Where the source operand is of word length, the dividend is originally stored in registers AX and DX, and after the division operation the integer quotient and remainder are returned in AX and DX respectively. For example, the instruction DIV 11, where AL=100 and AH=0, is equivalent to 100/11. The quotient, 9, is returned in AL and the remainder, 1, in AH. The instruction DIV 450, where AX=999 and DX=0, is equivalent to 999/450. The quotient, 2, is returned in AX and the remainder, 99, in DX.

ENTER (enter procedure)

Syntax: ENTER
Modes and object code format:

11001000	DATA LO	DATA HI	LEVEL

Mnemonic	Operation	Flags: O D I T S Z A P C
ENTER	Enter procedure	

Description: ENTER may be used at the beginning
of a procedure in high-level language
implementations to establish a stack frame for
nested procedures. The instruction specifies the
number of bytes required for stack storage for the
procedure, its lexical nesting level and the number
of stack frame pointers to be copied into the frame.
BP then points to the current stack frame pointer.
See also LEAVE.

ESC (escape)

Syntax: ESC opcode,addr
Modes and object code format:

11011nnn	MOD nnn R/M

Mnemonic	Operation	Flags: O D I T S Z A P C
ESC	Escape	

Description: ESC is used in conjunction with an
external co-processor, such as an I/O or a floating
point processor, and opens access to the required
addresses and operands by the external device. The
ESC mnemonic is followed by appropriate opcodes
for the co-processor and the instruction and by the
address of the required operand. *See also* WAIT.

HLT (halt)

Syntax: HLT
Modes and object code format:

11110100

Mnemonic	Operation	Flags: O D I T S Z A P C
HLT	Halt	

Description: HALT halts the processor until the reset line is activated, or a non-maskable interrupt is requested, or until a maskable interrupt is requested while interrupts are enabled.

IDIV (integer division)

Syntax: IDIV source
Modes and object code format:

1111011W	MOD 111 R/M

Mnemonic	Operation	Flags: O D I T S Z A P C
IDIV	Integer division	? ? ? ? ? ?

Description: IDIV is similar to DIV except that the division operation is performed with signed operands. Where the source operand is of byte length, the dividend is originally stored in registers AL and AH, and after the division operation the signed integer quotient and remainder are returned in AL and AH respectively. Where the source operand is of word length, the dividend is originally stored in registers AX and DX, and after the division operation the signed integer quotient and remainder are returned in AX and DX respectively. The remainder takes the sign of the dividend.

IMUL (integer multiply)

Syntax: IMUL source
Modes and object code format:

Reg. or mem.

1111011W	MOD 101 R/M

Imm.

011010S1	MOD REG R/M	DATA	DATA IF S=0

Mnemonic	Operation	Flags: O D I T S Z A P C
IMUL	Integer multiplication	A ? ? ? ? A

Description: IMUL multiplies an 8- or 16-bit source operand by the contents of the accumulator. A byte source is multiplied by AL with the product being returned in AH and AL. A word source is multiplied by AX with the product being returned in DX and AX. If the most significant halves of the product (AH or DX) contain significant digits, then the CF and OF flags are set; otherwise they are reset.

IN (input)

Syntax: IN acc,port
Modes and object code format:

Port specified by constant:

1110010W	PORT NO.

Port specified by DX:

1110110W

Mnemonic	Operation	Flags: O D I T S Z A P C
IN	Input	

Description: IN transfers data from a specified port
to either the AL or AX register, depending on
whether a byte or word value is required. The port
may be specified either directly, by means of a
single byte constant, or indirectly, by means of a
word value contained in the DX register.

INC (increment)

Syntax: INC dest
Modes and object code format:

Reg. or mem.:

1111111W	MOD 000 R/M

Reg:

01000REG

Mnemonic	Operation	Flags: O D I T S Z A P C
INC	Increment	A A A A A X

Description: INC increments the destination operand
by 1.

INS (Input string)

Syntax: INS acc,port
Modes and object code format:

From DX port:

0110110W

Repeated by count in CX:

11110010	0110110W

Mnemonic	Operation	Flags: O D I T S Z A P C
INS	Input string	

Description: INS passes a byte or word string from
an I/O port specified by DX to AL or AX, subject to
the privilege level of the task. If the operation is
prefixed by REP, the reiteration count is held in the
CX register. *See also* IN OUT and OUTS.

INT (interrupt)

Syntax: INT n (where n = range 0 to 255)
Modes and object code format:

Specified by type number:

11001101	TYPE NO.

Type 3:

11001100

Mnemonic	Operation	Flags: O D I T S Z A P C
INT	Interrupt	X 0 0

Description: INT initializes an interrupt procedure of
a type specified by the instruction, for example INT
5. The type value is used to access a vector table
which supplies CS and IP values for the appropriate
interrupt handling routine. The current environment
is saved on the stack prior to the initialization of the
interrupt routine. This is a 2-byte instruction with the
exception of INT 3, which is a 1-byte instruction
marking a breakpoint, for use with debugging
routines.

INTO (interrupt on overflow)

Syntax: INTO
Modes and object code format:

11001110

Mnemonic	Operation	Flags: O D I T S Z A P C
INTO	Interrupt on overflow	X 0 0

Description: INTO is used to generate a software interrupt dependent on the state of the OF flag. If OF is reset, then execution passes to the next instruction. If it is set, then SP is decremented by 2, the flags are stacked, IF and TF are reset, SP is further decremented by 2, CS is stacked, the data currently occupying address 12h is loaded into CS, SP is further decremented by 2, IP is stacked and finally, the data currently occupying address 10h is loaded into the IP register. *See also* IRET.

IRET (interrupt return)

Syntax: IRET
Modes and object code format:

11001111

Mnemonic	Operation	Flags: O D I T S Z A P C
IRET	Interrupt return	A A A A A A A A A

Description: IRET is used to return from an interrupt and retrieves IP, CS and the flags from the stack. *See also* INTO.

75

Jump instructions

Syntax: J(cond) [8__bit_signed__disp]
JMP 8__bit_signed__disp

Modes and object code format:

JA & JNBE:

01110111	DISP

JAE & JNB:

01110011	DISP

JB & JNAE:

01110010	DISP

JBE & JNA:

01110110	DISP

JC:

01110010	DISP

JCXZ:

11100011	DISP

JE & JZ:

01110100	DISP

JG & JNLE:

01111111	DISP

JGE & JNL:

01111101	DISP

JL & JNGE:

01111100	DISP

JLE & JNG:

01111110	DISP

JMP intra-segment direct:

11101001	DISP LO	DISP HI

JMP intra-segment direct (short):

11101011	DISP

JMP intra-segment indirect:

11111111	MOD 100 R/M

JMP inter-segment direct:

11101010	OFFSET LO	OFFSET HI
	SEG.LO	SEG.HI

JMP inter-segment indirect:

11111111	MOD 101 R/M

JNC:

01110011	DISP

JNE & JNZ:

01110101	DISP

JNO:

01110001	DISP

JNS:

01111001	DISP

JNP & JPO:

01111011	DISP

JO:

01110000	DISP

JP & JPE:

01111010	DISP

JS:

01111000	DISP

Mnemonic	Operation	Flags: O D I T S Z A P C
JA	Jump on above	
JNBE	Jump on not below or equal	
JAE	Jump on above or equal	
JNB	Jump on not below	
JB	Jump on below	
JNAE	Jump on not above or equal	
JBE	Jump on below or equal	
JNA	Jump on not above	
JC	Jump on carry	
JCXZ	Jump if CX=0	
JE	Jump on equal	
JZ	Jump on zero	
JG	Jump on greater than	
JNLE	Jump on not less or equal	
JGE	Jump on greater or equal	
JNL	Jump on not less	
JL	Jump on less	
JNGE	Jump on not greater or equal	
JLE	Jump on less or equal	
JNG	Jump on not greater than	
JMP	Unconditional jump	
JNC	Jump on not carry	
JNE	Jump on not equal	
JNZ	Jump on not zero	
JNO	Jump on not overflow	
JNS	Jump on not sign	
JNP	Jump on not parity	
JPO	Jump on parity odd	
JO	Jump on overflow	
JP	Jump on parity	
JPE	Jump on parity even	
JS	Jump on sign	

Description: JA transfers execution to a location calculated as the sum of the IP register plus an 8-bit signed displacement value which is sign extended to 16 bits. The jump is conditional upon (CF or ZF) = 0. JNBE is the same as JA

JAE transfers execution to a location calculated as the sum of the IP register plus an 8-bit signed displacement value which is sign extended to 16 bits. The jump is conditional upon CF = 0.

JNB is the same as JAE.

JB transfers execution to a location calculated as the sum of the IP register plus an 8-bit signed displacement value which is sign extended to 16 bits. The jump is conditional upon CF = 1.

JNAE is the same as JB.

JBE transfers execution to a location calculated as the sum of the IP register plus an 8-bit signed displacement value which is sign extended to 16 bits. The jump is conditional upon CF = 1 or ZF = 1.

JNA is the same as JBE.

JC transfers execution to a location calculated as the sum of the IP register plus an 8-bit signed displacement value which is sign extended to 16 bits. The jump is conditional upon CF = 1.

JCXZ transfers execution to a location calculated as the sum of the IP register plus an 8-bit signed displacement value which is sign extended to 16 bits. The jump is conditional upon CX = 0.

JE transfers execution to a location calculated as the sum of the IP register plus an 8-bit signed displacement value which is sign extended to 16 bits. The jump is conditional upon ZF = 1.

JZ is the same as JE.

JG transfers execution to a location calculated as the sum of the IP register plus an 8-bit signed displacement value which is sign extended to 16 bits. The jump is conditional upon ((SF xor OF)or ZF)=0.

JNLE is the same as JG.

JGE transfers execution to a location calculated as the sum of the IP register plus an 8-bit signed displacement value which is sign extended to 16 bits. The jump is conditional upon (SF xor OF)=0.

JNL is the same as JGE.

JL transfers execution to a location calculated as the sum of the IP register plus an 8-bit signed displacement value which is sign extended to 16 bits. The jump is conditional upon (SF xor OF)=1.

JNGE is the same as JL.

JLE transfers execution to a location calculated as the sum of the IP register plus an 8-bit signed displacement value which is sign extended to 16 bits. The jump is conditional upon ((SF xor OF) or ZF)=1.

JNG is the same as JLE.

JMP transfers execution unconditionally. For intra-segment jumps, the new address is a signed 8- or 16-bit displacement from the JMP instruction. For inter-segment jumps, the new address is again a displacement from the jump instruction but the new segment address must also be incorporated, as an extension word. This is loaded into the CS register during execution of JMP.

JNC transfers execution to a location calculated as the sum of the IP register plus an 8-bit signed displacement value which is sign extended to 16 bits. The jump is conditional upon $CF = 0$.

JNE transfers execution to a location calculated as the sum of the IP register plus an 8-bit signed displacement value which is sign extended to 16 bits. The jump is conditional upon $ZF = 0$.

JNZ is the same as JNE.

JNO transfers execution to a location calculated as the sum of the IP register plus an 8-bit signed displacement value which is sign extended to 16 bits. The jump is conditional upon $OF = 0$.

JNS transfers execution to a location calculated as the sum of the IP register plus an 8-bit signed displacement value which is sign extended to 16 bits. The jump is conditional upon $SF = 0$.

JNP transfers execution to a location calculated as the sum of the IP register plus an 8-bit signed displacement value which is sign extended to 16 bits. The jump is conditional upon $PF = 0$.

JPO is the same as JNP.

JO transfers execution to a location calculated as the sum of the IP register plus an 8-bit signed displacement value which is sign extended to 16 bits. The jump is conditional upon $OF = 1$.

JP transfers execution to a location calculated as the sum of the IP register plus an 8-bit signed displacement value which is sign extended to 16 bits. The jump is conditional upon $PF = 1$.

JPE is the same as JP.

JS transfers execution to a location calculated as the sum of the IP register plus an 8-bit signed displacement value which is sign extended to 16 bits. The jump is conditional upon SF=1.

Note that in conditional jumping operations the terms *above* and *below* refer to the relation between two unsigned integers, and *greater* and *less* refer to the relation between signed integers. In other words, one unsigned number may be above or below another in value (e.g. 10 is above 6), while a signed number may be greater or lesser than another (e.g. 10 greater than −10).

LAHF (load AH from flags)

Syntax: LAHF
Modes and object code format:

10011111

Mnemonic	Operation	Flags: O D I T S Z A P C
LAHF	Load AH from flags	

Description: LAHF loads bits 7, 6, 4, 2 and 0 of register AH with the contents of the SF, ZF, AF, PF and CF flags respectively. The contents of the remaining bits are not defined.

LAR (load access rights)

Syntax: LAR dest,source
Modes and object code format:

00001111	00000010	MOD REG R/M

Mnemonic	Operation	Flags: O D I T S Z A P C
LAR	Load access rights	

Description: LAR is a protection control instruction
which loads the high byte of a register with the
access rights data of a descriptor, taken either from
memory or from a register.

LDS (load pointer using DS)

Syntax: LDS dest,source
Modes and object code format:

11000101	MOD REG R/M

Mnemonic	Operation	Flags: O D I T S Z A P C
LDS	Load pointer using DS	

Description: LDS transfers 4 bytes from memory to
two 16-bit registers, one of which must be DS.
Therefore, if a pre-defined pointer value is stored in
memory it can be loaded into the data segment
register and an offset register in one operation,
prior to the execution of an operation requiring
indirect addressing.

LEA (load effective address)

Syntax: LEA dest,source
Modes and object code format:

| 10001101 | MOD REG R/M |

Mnemonic	Operation	Flags: O D I T S Z A P C
LEA	Load effective address	

Description: LEA transfers a 16-bit source operand
in memory to a 16-bit destination register. The
register may then be used as an offset by other
instructions for accessing target data.

LEAVE (leave procedure)

Syntax: LEAVE
Modes and object code format:

| 11001001 |

Mnemonic	Operation	Flags: O D I T S Z A P C
LEAVE	Leave procedure	

Description: LEAVE reverses the actions of the
ENTER instruction, relinquishing a nested task stack
frame.

LES (load pointer using ES)

Syntax: LES dest,source
Modes and object code format:

11000100	MOD REG R/M

Mnemonic	Operation	Flags: O D I T S Z A P C
LES	Load pointer using ES	

Description: LES transfers 4 bytes from memory to
two 16-bit registers, one of which must be ES.
Therefore, if a pre-defined pointer value is stored in
memory it can be loaded into the extra segment
register and an offset register in one operation,
prior to the execution of an operation requiring
indirect addressing.

LGDT (load global descriptor table register)

Syntax: LGDT source
Modes and object code format:

00001111	00000001	MOD 010 R/M

Mnemonic	Operation	Flags: O D I T S Z A P C
LGDT	Load GDTR	

Description: LGDT is a protection control instruction
which loads the global descriptor table register
(GDTR) with 6 bytes of source data, consisting of
the location and length of the global descriptor
table. The instruction specifies the location of the
source data.

LIDT (load interrupt descriptor table register)

Syntax: LIDT source
Modes and object code format:

00001111	00000001	MOD 011 R/M

Mnemonic	Operation	Flags: O D I T S Z A P C
LIDT	Load IDTR	

Description: LIDT is a protection control instruction which loads the interrupt descriptor table register (IDTR) with 6 bytes of source data, consisting of the location and length of the interrupt descriptor table. The instruction specifies the location of the source data.

LLDT (load local descriptor table register)

Syntax: LLDT source
Modes and object code format:

00001111	00000000	MOD 010 R/M

Mnemonic	Operation	Flags: O D I T S Z A P C
LLDT	Load LDTR	

Description: LLDT is a protection control instruction which loads the local descriptor table register (LDTR) with a selector (contained in memory or a register) for a local descriptor table listed within the global descriptor table.

LMSW (load machine status word register)

Syntax: LMSW source
Modes and object code format:

00001111	00000001	MOD 110 R/M

Mnemonic	Operation	Flags: O D I T S Z A P C
LMSW	Load MSW	

Description: LMSW is a protection control instruction which loads the machine status word register (MSW) with source data taken from memory or a register. This data includes the PE bit, which initiates protected mode operation.

LOCK (lock bus)

Syntax: LOCK
Modes and object code format:

11110000

Mnemonic	Operation	Flags: O D I T S Z A P C
LOCK	Lock bus	

Description: LOCK is an instruction used in resource-sharing applications to ensure that memory is not accessed simultaneously by more than one processor. When an instruction is prefixed by LOCK, the processor immediately locks the bus by asserting a signal on the LOCK pin. Access by other processors is then prohibited until the following instruction has been executed.

In some cases, where necessary, the processor's LOCK pin is asserted automatically without the use of a LOCK prefix.

LODS (load string)

Syntax: LODS source
Modes and object code format:

1010110W

Mnemonic	Operation	Flags: O D I T S Z A P C
LODS	Load byte or word string	

Description: LODS is used to copy a byte or word string from a location addressed by the SI index offset into either AL or AX. Following the transfer, SI is either incremented or decremented, depending on whether the DF flag is 0 or 1.

LOOP (loop if CX non-zero)

Syntax: LOOP signed__byte
Modes and object code format:

11100010	DISP

Mnemonic	Operation	Flags: O D I T S Z A P C
LOOP	Loop if CX non-zero	

Description: LOOP decrements the CX register by 1 and if it is greater than zero, transfers execution to a location calculated as the sum of the IP register plus an 8-bit displacement value, sign extended to 16 bits. If CX equals zero, then execution passes on to the following instruction.

LOOPE and LOOPZ (loop while equal and loop while zero)

Syntax: LOOPE signed__byte   LOOPZ signed__byte
Modes and object code format:

LOOPE and LOOPZ

11100001	DISP

Mnemonic	Operation	Flags: O D I T S Z A P C
LOOPE	Loop while equal	
LOOPZ	Loop while zero	

Description: LOOPE and LOOPZ function
identically. They decrement the CX register by 1
and if it is other than zero, and ZF=1, they transfer
execution to a location calculated as the sum of the
IP register plus an 8-bit displacement value sign
extended to 16 bits. If CX or ZF equal zero, then
execution passes on to the following instruction.

LOOPNE and LOOPNZ (loop while not equal and loop while not zero)

Syntax: LOOPNE signed__byte   LOOPNZ signed__byte
Modes and object code format:

LOOPNE & LOOPNZ

11100000	DISP

Mnemonic	Operation	Flags: O D I T S Z A P C
LOOPNE	Loop while not equal	
LOOPNZ	Loop while not zero	

Description: LOOPNE and LOOPNZ function identically. They decrement the CX register by 1 and if it is other than zero, and ZF=0, they transfer execution to a location calculated as the sum of the IP register plus an 8-bit displacement value sign extended to 16 bits. Otherwise execution passes on to the following instruction.

LSL (load segment limit)

Syntax: LSL dest,source
Modes and object code format:

00001111	00000011	MOD REG R/M

Mnemonic	Operation	Flags: O D I T S Z A P C
LSL	Load segment limit	A

Description: LSL is a protection control instruction which loads a segment limit value from a descriptor into a register, subject to privilege rights. If the operation is successful, the ZF flag is set.

LTR (load task register)

Syntax: LTR source
Modes and object code format:

00001111	00000000	MOD 011 R/M

Mnemonic	Operation	Flags: O D I T S Z A P C
LTR	Load task register	

Description: LTR is a protection control instruction
which loads the task register (TR) with the selector
for one of the task state segments which are listed
in the global descriptor table.

MOV (move)

Syntax: MOV dest,source
Modes and object code format:

Reg. or mem. to or from reg.:

100010DW	MOD REG R/M

Imm. to reg. or mem.:

1100011W	MOD 000 R/M	DATA	DATA IF W=1

Imm. to reg.:

1011WREG	DATA	DATA IF W=1

Mem. to acc.:

1010000W	ADDR.LO	ADDR.HI

Acc. to mem.:

1010001W	ADDR.LO	ADDR.HI

Reg. or mem. to segment reg.:

10001110	MOD 0 REG R/M

Segment reg. to reg. or mem.:

10001100	MOD 0 REG R/M

Mnemonic Operation	Flags: O D I T S Z A P C
MOV Move byte or word	

Description: MOV transfers 8- or 16-bit data from a source to a destination.

92

MOVS (move string)

Syntax: MOVS dest__string,source__string
Modes and object code format:

1010010W

Mnemonic	Operation	Flags: O D I T S Z A P C
MOVS	Move byte or word	

Description: MOVS copies 8- or 16-bit string data
from a source to a destination. The source and
destination are addressed by SI and DI respectively
and both these registers are either incremented or
decremented, according to the status of the DF
flag, after the data has been transferred. *See also*
REP for repeat moves.

MUL (multiply)

Syntax: MUL source
Modes and object code format:

1111011W	MOD 100 R/M

Mnemonic	Operation	Flags: O D I T S Z A P C
MUL	Multiply	A ? ? ? ? A

Description: MUL is used to multiply the unsigned
contents of the accumulator and a specified source
operand. Where the source is a byte, AL is the
accumulator and the product is stored in AH and
AL. The CF and OF flags are set if AH contains a
significant value. Where the source is a word, AX is
the accumulator and the product is stored in DX
and AX. The CF and OF flags are set if DX contains
a significant value.

NEG (negate)

Syntax: NEG dest
Modes and object code format:

| 1111011W | MOD 011 R/M |

Mnemonic	Operation	Flags:	O	D	I	T	S	Z	A	P	C
NEG	Negate		A				A	A	A	A	A

Description: NEG subtracts a destination operand from zero, storing the two's complement result in the destination.

NOP (no operation)

Syntax: NOP
Modes and object code format:

| 10010000 |

Mnemonic	Operation	Flags:	O	D	I	T	S	Z	A	P	C
NOP	No operation										

Description: NOP has no effect.

NOT (logical NOT)

Syntax: NOT dest
Modes and object code format:

| 1111011W | MOD 010 R/M |

Mnemonic	Operation	Flags: O D I T S Z A P C
NOT	Logical NOT operation	

Description: NOT performs a logical NOT
operation on the specified destination operand,
inverting each of its bits.

OR (logical OR)

Syntax: OR dest,source
Modes and object code format:

Reg. or mem. and reg. to reg. or mem.:

| 000010DW | MOD REG R/M |

Imm. to reg. or mem.:

| 1000000W | MOD 001 R/M | DATA | DATA IF W=1 |

Imm. to acc.:

| 0000110W | DATA | DATA if W=1 |

Mnemonic	Operation	Flags: O D I T S Z A P C
OR	Logical OR operation	0 A A ? A 0

Description: OR performs a logical OR operation
between specified source and destination operands.
For each of the corresponding bits in the source
and destination operands the result is 1 if either of
the bits are set or zero if neither are set.

OUT (output)

Syntax: OUT port,acc
Modes and object code format:

Port specified by constant

1110011W	PORT

Port specified by DX

1110111W

Mnemonic Operation	Flags: O D I T S Z A P C
OUT Output to port	

Description: OUT is used to transfer data from AL
or AX to an output port specified either by a single
byte constant or by a word value stored in register
DX.

OUTS (output string)

Syntax: OUTS
Modes and object code format:

To DX port:

0110111W

Repeated by count in CX:

11110010	0110111W

Mnemonic	Operation	Flags: O D I T S Z A P C
OUTS	Output string	

Description: OUTS passes a byte or word string
from AL or AX to an I/O port specified by DX,
subject to the privilege level of the task. If the
operation is prefixed by REP, the reiteration count is
held in the CX register. *See also* OUT, IN and INS.

POP (pop from stack)

Syntax: POP dest
Modes and object code format:

Reg. or mem.:

10001111	MOD 000 R/M

Reg.:

01011REG

Segment reg.:

000REG111

Mnemonic Operation	Flags: O D I T S Z A P C
POP Pop data from stack	

Description: POP transfers the word value currently stored on top of the stack into a specified destination. The stack pointer (SP) is then incremented by two. *See also* PUSH.

POPA (pop all)

Syntax: POPA
Modes and object code format:

01100001

Mnemonic Operation	Flags: O D I T S Z A P C
POPA Pop all registers	

Description: POPA pops the contents of all the registers from the stack, excluding SP. *See also* PUSHA

POPF (pop flags)

Syntax: POPF
Modes and object code format:

10011101

Mnemonic	Operation	Flags: O D I T S Z A P C
POPF	Pop flags from stack	A A A A A A A A A

Description: POPF is used to transfer the word currently stored on top of the stack into the flag register. The stack pointer (SP) is then incremented by two. *See also* PUSHF.

PUSH (push to stack)

Syntax: PUSH source
Modes and object code format:

Reg. or mem.:

11111111	MOD 110 R/M

Reg.:

01010REG

Segment reg.:

000REG110

Imm.:

011010S0	DATA	DATA if S=0

Mnemonic	Operation	Flags: O D I T S Z A P C
PUSH	Push source on to stack	

Description: PUSH decrements the stack pointer by two and transfers a word from a specified source on to the top of the stack. *See also* POP.

99

PUSHA (push all)

Syntax: PUSHA
Modes and object code format:

01100000

Mnemonic	Operation	Flags: O D I T S Z A P C
PUSHA	Push all registers	

Description: PUSHA saves the contents of all the registers on the stack. *See also* POPA.

PUSHF (push flags)

Syntax: PUSHF
Modes and object code format:

10011100

Mnemonic	Operation	Flags: O D I T S Z A P C
PUSHF	Push flags on to stack	

Description: PUSHF decrements the stack pointer by two and transfers the contents of the flags register on to the top of the stack. *See also* POPF.

RCL (rotate left with carry)

Syntax: RCL dest,counter__value
Modes and object code format:

by 1 or CL:

110100VW	MOD 010 R/M

Imm. >1:

1100000W	MOD 010 R/M	count

Mnemonic	Operation	Flags: O D I T S Z A P C
RCL	rotate left with carry (1)	A X X X X A
RCL	rotate left with carry (CL)	? X X X X A
RCL	rotate left with carry (>1)	? X X X X A

Description: RCL is used to rotate the bits contained in a specified destination operand to the left with a counter operand being used to specify the number of times the operation is performed. For example, RCL AL,1 rotates the bits contained in AL once to the left. The count may be either an immediate value or one held in the CL register. During each rotation the contents of the CF flag are transferred to the low-order bit of the destination while the high-order bit is transferred to the CF flag. If the count value equals 1 and the high-order bit differs from its previous value, then OF is set; otherwise it is reset.

RCR (rotate right with carry)

Syntax: RCR dest,counter__value
Modes and object code format:

By 1 or CL:

110100VW	MOD 011 R/M

Imm. >1:

1100000W	MOD 011 R/M	count

Mnemonic	Operation	Flags:	O	D	I	T	S	Z	A	P	C
RCR	Rotate right with carry (1)		A					X	X	X	X	A
RCR	Rotate right with carry (CL)		?					X	X	X	X	A
RCR	Rotate right with carry (>1)		?					X	X	X	X	A

Description: RCR is used to rotate the bits contained in a specified destination operand to the right with a counter operand being used to specify the number of times the operation is performed. For example, RCR AL,1 rotates the bits contained in AL once to the right. The count may be either an immediate value or one held in the CL register. During each rotation the contents of the CF flag are transferred to the high-order bit of the destination while the low-order bit is transferred to the CF flag. If the count value equals 1 and the high-order bit differs from its previous value, then OF is set, otherwise it is reset.

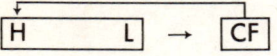

Repeat operations: REP, REPE, REPZ, REPNE, REPNZ

Syntax: REP (INSTR) dest,source
REPNE (INSTR)
REPE (INSTR)
REPNZ (INSTR)
REPZ (INSTR)

Modes and object code format:

1111001Z

Mnemonic	Operation	Flags: O D I T S Z A P C
REP	Repeat	
REPE	Repeat while equal	
REPZ	Repeat while zero	
REPNE	Repeat while non-equal	
REPNZ	Repeat while non-zero	

Description: REP is an optional prefix to the MOVS, STOS, INS and OUTS commands and causes these instructions to be repeated until the CX flag equals zero (end of a string). Thus REP MOVS dest,source effectively becomes a memory to memory block transfer instruction, while REP STOS dest__string repeatedly transfers data from either AX or AL to a sequence of memory locations addressed by DI. *See also* MOVS and STOS.

REPE and REPZ operate in the same way as REP and are used as a prefix to the CMPS and SCAS instructions when a repeat operation is required. REPE CMPS dest__string,source__string will compare consecutive strings until either the end of the string is reached (CX=0) or the compared strings are unequal (ZF=0). REPE SCAS dest__string subtracts

a sequence of data from the contents of AX or AL
until either the end of string is reached (CX=0) or
the operands are unequal ZF=0.

REPNE and REPNZ operate in a similar way to
REPE and REPZ except that the repeat operation
continues until either the end of the string is
reached (CX=0) or the operands are equal
(ZF=1).

RET (return from subroutine)

Syntax: RET disp
Modes and object code format:

Intra-segment:

11000011

Intra-segment plus imm. to SP:

11000010	DATA LO	DATA HI

Inter-segment:

11001011

Inter-segment plus imm. to SP:

11001010	DATA LO	DATA HI

Mnemonic	Operation	Flags: O D I T S Z A P C
RET	Return from subroutine	

Description: RET is used to return from a
subroutine. If the CALL and the subroutine are
within the same segment (intra-segment call), then
the previous IP value is popped off the stack and
execution is recommenced from the address
following the CALL instruction. If the CALL and the
subroutine are in different segments (inter-segment

call), then the previous IP value and the previous segment register value are popped from the stack.

RET disp is the same as RET except that a displacement constant is specified, which is added to the value of the stack pointer.

ROL (rotate left)

Syntax: ROL dest,counter__value
Modes and object code format:

By 1 or CL:

110100VW	MOD 000 R/M

Imm. >1:

1100000W	MOD 000 R/M	count

Mnemonic	Operation	Flags: O D I T S Z A P C
ROL	Rotate left (1)	A X X X X A
ROL	Rotate left (CL)	? X X X X A
ROL	Rotate left (>1)	? X X X X A

Description: ROL is used to rotate the destination operand to the left, with a count operand being used to specify the number of times the rotation is performed. The count may be either an immediate value or one held in the CL register. On each rotation the high order bit is transferred to the least significant bit position and into CF. If the count value equals 1 and the high-order bit differs from its previous value, then OF is set; otherwise it is reset.

105

ROR (rotate right)

Syntax: ROR dest,counter value
Modes and object code format:

By 1 or CL:

110100VW	MOD 001 R/M

Imm. >1:

1100000W	MOD 001 R/M	count

Mnemonic	Operation	Flags: O D I T S Z A P C
ROR	Rotate right (1)	A X X X X A
ROR	Rotate right (CL)	? X X X X A
ROR	Rotate right (>1)	? X X X X A

Description: ROR is used to rotate the destination
operand to the right, with a count operand being
used to specify the number of times the rotation is
performed. If the count value is 1 it may be
specified as a constant; otherwise CL is used to hold
the count. On each rotation the low-order bit is
transferred to the most significant bit position and
into CF. If the count value equals 1 and the high-
order bit differs from its previous value, then OF is
set, otherwise it is reset.

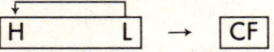

SAHF (store AH in flags register)

Syntax: SAHF
Modes and object code format:

```
10011110
```

Mnemonic	Operation	Flags: O D I T S Z A P C
SAHF	Store AH in flags register	X A A A A A

Description: SAHF is used to alter the contents of the S, Z, A, P and C flags, using bits transferred from bits 7, 6, 4, 2 and 0 of register AH:

7	6		4		2		0	Register AH
↓	↓		↓		↓		↓	
SF	ZF		AF		PF		CF	Flags register

SAL & SHL (shift left arithmetic & logical)

Syntax: SAL dest,counter__value
       SHL dest,counter__value
Modes and object code format:

By 1 or CL:

```
110100VW   MOD 100 R/M
```

Imm. >1:

```
1100000W   MOD 100 R/M   count
```

Mnemonic	Operation	Flags: O D I T S Z A P C
SAL/SHL	Shift arith./log. left (1)	A A A ? A A
SAL/SHL	Shift arith./log. left (CL)	? A A ? A A
SAL/SHL	Shift arith./log. left (>1)	? A A ? A A

Description: SAL and SHL are used to rotate the destination operand to the left, with a count operand being used to specify the number of times the rotation is performed. The count may be either an immediate value or one held in the CL register. On each rotation a zero is placed in the least significant bit position and if the count value equals 1 and the most significant bit differs from its previous value, then OF is set; otherwise it is reset.

SAR & SHR (shift right arithmetic & logical)

Syntax: SAR dest,counter__value
SHR dest,counter__value
Modes and object code format:

SHR by 1 or CL:

110100VW	MOD 101 R/M

SHR imm. >1:

1100000W	MOD 101 R/M	count

SAR by 1 or CL:

110100VW	MOD 111 R/M

SAR imm. >1:

1100000W	MOD 111 R/M	count

108

Mnemonic	Operation	Flags:	O	D	I	T	S	Z	A	P	C
SAR	Shift arithmetic right (1)		A				A	A	?	A	A
SAR	Shift arithmetic right (CL)		?				A	A	?	A	A
SAR	Shift arithmetic right (>1)		?				A	A	?	A	A
SHR	Shift logical right (1)		A				A	A	?	A	A
SHR	Shift logical right (CL)		?				A	A	?	A	A
SHR	Shift logical right (>1)		?				A	A	?	A	A

Description: SAR is used to rotate the destination operand to the right, with a count operand being used to specify the number of times the rotation is performed. If the count value is 1 it may be specified as a constant; otherwise CL is used to hold the count. On each rotation the least significant bit is discarded while the most significant (sign) bit is replaced by a value equal to its original value.

SHR also rotates to the right, as with SAR, but on each rotation a zero is placed in the most significant bit position. If the count value equals 1 and the high-order bit differs from its previous value, then OF = 1.

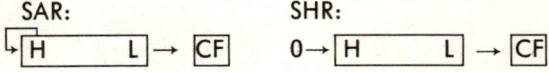

SBB (subtract with borrow)

Syntax: SBB dest,source
Modes and object code format:

Reg. or mem. and reg. to reg. or mem.:

000110DW	MODREG R/M

Imm. from reg. or mem.:

100000SW	MOD 011 R/M	DATA	DATA IF S:W=01

Imm. from acc.:

0001110W	DATA	DATA IF W=1

Mnemonic	Operation	Flags: O D I T S Z A P C
SBB	Subtract with borrow	A A A A A

Description: Subtracts a signed or unsigned source
operand from a signed or unsigned destination,
then subtracts 1 from the result if CF=1. The result
is returned in the destination.

SCAS (scan string)

Syntax: SCAS dest__string
Modes and object code format:

1010111W

Mnemonic	Operation	Flags: O D I T S Z A P C
SCAS	Scan string	A A A A A A

Description: SCAS is used to subtract a destination string, addressed by a DI register, from either AX or AL. Neither the source nor the destination values are altered but the A, C, O, P, S and Z flags are affected. After the operation, DI is either incremented or decremented, according to the condition of the DF flag, to point to the address of the next string element in sequence. *See also* REPE, REPZ, REPNE and REPNZ.

SMSW (store machine status word)

Syntax: SMSW dest
Modes and object code format:

000011111	00000001	MOD 100 R/M

Mnemonic	Operation	Flags: O D I T S Z A P C
SMSW	Store MSW	

Description: SMSW is a protection control instruction which stores the contents of the machine status word register in memory or in a register.

SGDT (store global descriptor table register)

Syntax: SGDT dest
Modes and object code format:

00001111	00000001	MOD 000 R/M

Mnemonic	Operation	Flags: O D I T S Z A P C
SGDT	Store GDTR	

Description: SGDT is a protection control instruction which stores the contents of the global descriptor table register (GDTR) in memory or in a register.

SIDT (store interrupt descriptor table reg.)

Syntax: SIDT dest
Modes and object code format:

00001111	00000001	MOD 001 R/M

Mnemonic	Operation	Flags: O D I T S Z A P C
SIDT	Store IDTR	

Description: SIDT is a protection control instruction which stores the contents of the interrupt descriptor table register (IDTR) in memory or in a register.

SLDT (store local descriptor table reg.)

Syntax: SLDT dest
Modes and object code format:

00001111	00000000	MOD 000 R/M

Mnemonic	Operation	Flags: O D I T S Z A P C
SLDT	Store LDTR	

Description: SLDT is a protection control instruction
which stores the contents of the local descriptor
table register (LDTR) in a register or in memory.

STC (set carry flag)

Syntax: STC
Modes and object code format:

11111001

Mnemonic	Operation	Flags: O D I T S Z A P C
STC	Set carry flag	X X X X X 1

Description: STC sets the CF flag.

STD (set direction flag)

Syntax: STD
Modes and object code format:

11111101

Mnemonic	Operation	Flags: O D I T S Z A P C
STD	Set direction flag	1 X X

Description: STC sets the DF flag. When DF is set the string instructions autodecrement the relevant index registers (SI and/or DI) and when DF is reset the string instructions autoincrement them.

STI (set interrupt enable flag)

Syntax: STI
Modes and object code format:

11111011

Mnemonic	Operation	Flags: O D I T S Z A P C
STI	Set interrupt enable flag	X 1 X

Description: STI sets the IF flag, enabling the recognition of maskable interrupt requests.

STOS (store string)

Syntax: STOS
Modes and object code format:

1010101W

Mnemonic	Operation	Flags: O D I T S Z A P C
STOS	Store string	

Description: STOS transfers a source operand, contained in either AX or AL, to a destination addressed by DI. After the operation, DI is incremented to point to the address of the next string element in sequence if DF=0 or decremented if DF=1.

STR (store task register)

Syntax: STR dest
Modes and object code format:

00001111	00000000	MOD 001 R/M

Mnemonic	Operation	Flags: O D I T S Z A P C
STR	Store TR	

Description: STR is a protection control instruction which stores the contents of the task register (TR) in memory or in a register.

SUB (subtract)

Syntax: SUB dest,source
Modes and object code format:

Reg. or mem. and reg. to reg. or mem.:

001010DW	MOD REG R/M

Imm. from reg. or mem.:

100000SW	MOD 101 R/M	DATA	DATA IF S:W=01

Imm. from acc.:

0010110W	DATA	DATA IF W=1

Mnemonic	Operation	Flags: O D I T S Z A P C
SUB	Subtract	A A A A A A

Description: SUB subtracts a source from a
destination operand with the result being placed in
the destination. The source and destination may be
signed or unsigned.

TEST (logical comparison)

Syntax: TEST dest,source
Modes and object code format:

Reg. or mem. and reg.:

1000010W	MOD REG R/M

Imm. and reg. or mem.:

1111011W	MOD 000 R/M	DATA	DATA IF W=1

Imm. and acc.:

1010100W	DATA	DATA IF W=1

Mnemonic	Operation	Flags: O D I T S Z A P C
TEST	Test operands	0 A A ? A 0

Description: TEST performs an AND operation between the source and destination operands without altering either. The flags are affected by the operation.

VERR (verify read access)

Syntax: VERR seg
Modes and object code format:

00001111	00000000	MOD 100 R/M

Mnemonic	Operation	Flags: O D I T S Z A P C
VERR	Verify read access	A

Description: A segment, specified by a selector value in the instruction, is verified for read protection. ZF is set if the segment may be read, otherwise reset.

117

VERW (verify write access)

Syntax: VERW seg
Modes and object code format:

| 00001111 | 00000000 | MOD 101 R/M |

Mnemonic	Operation	Flags: O D I T S Z A P C
VERW	Verify write access	A

Description: A segment, specified by a selector value in the instruction, is verified for write protection. ZF is set if the segment may be written to; otherwise reset.

WAIT

Syntax: WAIT
Modes and object code format:

| 10011011 |

Mnemonic	Operation	Flags: O D I T S Z A P C
WAIT	Wait until test line active	

Description: WAIT causes the processor to wait until a signal has been detected on the TEST pin. This occurs, for example, when a co-processor has completed an operation and signals its completion to the 80286. An ESC instruction, for passing an operand to a co-processor, may be preceded by a WAIT instruction, thus synchronizing the actions of the CPU and the slave processor so that ESC only becomes operative when the WAIT instruction has provided a 'ready' signal.

XCHG (exchange)

Syntax: XCHG dest,source
Modes and object code format:

Reg. or mem. with reg.:

1000011W	MOD REG R/M

Reg. with acc.:

10010REG

Mnemonic	Operation	Flags: O D I T S Z A P C
XCHG	Exchange source and destination	

Description: XCHG exchanges the contents of the source and destination operands.

XLAT (translate)

Syntax: XLAT table
Modes and object code format:

11010111

Mnemonic	Operation	Flags: O D I T S Z A P C
XLAT	Translate	

Description: XLAT is used for translating a byte in the AL register to a byte taken from a translation table. The data is taken from an address in the table corresponding to BX+AL, where BX is a pointer to the beginning of the table and AL is an index variable. Therefore, if AL originally contains 10, its value will be replaced by a byte from a location in the table addressed by BX+10.

XOR (exclusive OR)

Syntax: XOR dest, source
Modes and object code format:

Reg. or mem. and reg. to reg. or mem.:

001100DW	MOD REG R/M

Imm. to reg or mem.:

1000000W	MOD 110 R/M	DATA	DATA IF W=1

Imm. to acc.:

0011010W	DATA	DATA IF W=1

Mnemonic	Operation	Flags: O D I T S Z A P C
XOR	Exclusive OR operation	

Description: XOR performs an exclusive OR
operation between a destination and a source
operand with the result being returned in the
destination. For each of the corresponding bits in
the two operands the result is 1 if either but not
both of the bits are set; otherwise zero.

Instructions by Category

General purpose

BOUND	Detect value out of range
ENTER	Enter procedure
LEAVE	Leave procedure
MOV	Move
NOP	No operation
PUSH	Push to stack
PUSHA	Push all registers
POP	Pop from stack
POPA	Pop all registers
XCHG	Exchange
XLAT	Translate

I/O

IN   Input
OUT   Output

Address loading

LEA   Load effective address
LDS   Load pointer using DS
LES   Load pointer using ES

Flag storage and retrieval

LAHF   Load AH from flags
POPF   Pop flags
PUSHF   Push flags
SAHF   Store AH in flags register

Arithmetic

Addition
AAA   ASCII adjust for addition
ADC   Add with carry
ADD   Add
DAA   Decimal adjust for addition
INC   Increment

Subtraction
AAS   ASCII adjust for subtraction
CMP   Comparison
DAS   Decimal adjust for subtraction
DEC   Decrement
NEG   Negate
SBB   Subtract with borrow
SUB   Subtract

Multiplication
AAM   ASCII adjust for multiply
IMUL   Integer multiply
MUL   Unsigned multiply

Division
AAD   ASCII adjust for division
CBW   Convert byte to word
CWD   Convert word to double word
DIV   Unsigned division
IDIV   Integer divide

String operations

CMPS   Compare string
INS   Input string
LODS   Load string
MOVS   Move string
OUTS   Output string
REP   Repeat
REPE   Repeat while equal
REPNE   Repeat while not equal

REPNZ	Repeat while not zero
REPZ	Repeat while zero
SCAS	Scan string
STOS	Store string

Logical operations

AND	Logical and
NOT	Logical not
OR	Logical or
TEST	Logical comparison
XOR	Logical xor

Shift and rotate operations

RCL	Rotate left with carry
RCR	Rotate right with carry
ROL	Rotate left
ROR	Rotate right
SAL	Shift arithmetic left
SAR	Shift arithmetic right
SHL	Shift logical left
SHR	Shift logical right

Flag setting and clearing operations

CLC	Clear carry flag
CLD	Clear direction flag
CLI	Clear interrupt enable flag
CMC	Complement carry flag
CTS	Clear task switched flag
STC	Set carry flag
STD	Set direction flag
STI	Set interrupt enable flag

Processor control

ESC	Escape to co-processor
HLT	Halt pending interrupt or reset
LOCK	Lock bus
WAIT	Wait until test line active

Control transfer operations

Unconditional
CALL	Call subroutine
JMP	Jump
RET	Return from subroutine

Conditional
JA	Jump on above
JAE	Jump on above or equal
JB	Jump on below
JBE	Jump on below or equal
JC	Jump on carry
JCXZ	Jump if CX=0
JE	Jump on equal

JG	Jump on greater than
JGE	Jump on greater or equal
JL	Jump on less
JLE	Jump on less or equal
JNA	Jump on not above
JNAE	Jump on not above or equal
JNB	Jump on not below
JNBE	Jump on not below or equal
JNC	Jump on not carry
JNE	Jump on not equal
JNG	Jump on not greater than
JNGE	Jump on not greater or equal
JNL	Jump on not less
JNLE	Jump on not less or equal
JNO	Jump on not overflow
JNS	Jump on not sign
JNP	Jump on not parity
JNZ	Jump on not zero
JO	Jump on overflow
JP	Jump on parity even
JPE	Jump on parity equal
JPO	Jump on parity odd
JS	Jump on sign
JZ	Jump on zero

Loop control

JCXZ	Jump if CX (counter) $=0$
LOOP	Loop
LOOPE	Loop if equal
LOOPNE	Loop if not equal
LOOPNZ	Loop if not zero
LOOPZ	Loop if zero

Interrupts

INT	Interrupt
INTO	Interrupt if overflow
IRET	Interrupt return

Protection control

ARPL	Adjust requested privilege level
LAR	Load access rights
LGDT	Load global descriptor table register
LIDT	Load interrupt descriptor table register
LLDT	Load local descriptor table register
LMSW	Load machine status word
LSL	Load segment limit
LTR	Load task register
SGDT	Store global descriptor table register
SIDT	Store interrupt descriptor table register
SLDT	Store local descriptor table register
SMSW	Store machine status word
STR	Store task register
VERR	Verify read access
VERW	Verify write access

Index

Printed in Great Britain
by Amazon

24360506R00064

If you have enjoyed the Formula 1 jokes presented in this book, we would like to ask you to share a review on Amazon.

Your opinion is extremely valuable to us and to other Formula 1 enthusiasts who are looking to be entertained and have a laugh about this sport.

We understand that leaving a comment can be a tedious process, but we kindly ask you to take a few minutes of your time to share your thoughts and opinions with us.

Your support is greatly important to us and helps us continue creating quality content for the fans of this incredible sport.

We sincerely appreciate your support in advance and hope that you have enjoyed this book as much as we have enjoyed creating it.

May speed always be on your side!

★ ★ ★ ★ ★

101

Famous quotes.

- Graham Hill: "The car is an extension of my body."

- Kimi Raikkonen: "What do Finns do in their free time? Go fishing and make love in the summer. Fishing is really bad in winter."

- Pedro de la Rosa: "I worked very hard, very hard to get here. Sacrifices? None. It was hard, but not sacrificed. Sacrifice is doing something you don't want to do."

- Colin Chapman: "Rules are meant to be obeyed by fools and interpreted by the wise."

- John Surtees: "If anyone took the Lotus and pushed it to the limit, it would break. But Jim Clark understood it."

- Enzo Ferrari: "I don't sell cars, I sell engines. I give away cars because you have to put the engine somewhere."

100

Famous quotes.

- Kimi Raikkonen: "Formula 1 would be a paradise without the press."

- Jackie Stewart: "Is your dad a driver? When is he going to kill himself? That's what they asked my children at school."

- Colin Chapman: "Weight is the enemy. More power makes you faster on the straights, less weight makes you faster everywhere."

- Jim Clark: "When I want to go faster, I don't run more, I focus more."

- Sebastian Vettel: "If you want to have a friend in the paddock, bring your dog."

- Enzo Ferrari: "My cars win races, and the drivers lose them."

99

Famous quotes.

- Gilles Villeneuve: "The perfect race for me is: I achieve pole position at the last moment, I have a problem at the start, I climb up from the last position, and I get to first place in the last corner."

- Damon Hill: "Winning is everything. If you finish second, only your wife and the dog remember it."

- Alain Prost: "The difference between Ayrton Senna and me is that I believe in God and he thinks he is God."

- Eddie Irvine: "Winning in F1 is like having sex with the ten most beautiful women in the world."

- Enzo Ferrari: "I build sports cars, you build tractors. Stick to them." [Said to Ferruccio Lamborghini]

- Nelson Piquet: "I am used to winning championships, and Mansell is used to losing them."

98

Famous quotes.

- Nelson Piquet: "Fear is part of the game, but traffic in Brazil is much more dangerous than an F1 circuit."

- Alberto Ascari: "After an accident, the best thing is to get back behind the wheel as soon as possible."

- James Hunt: "I don't think I'm going to die lying in a bed."

- Niki Lauda: "I never dwell in the past. I only take the acquired experience, especially the bad experience, so as not to repeat it."

- Ayrton Senna: "I don't know how to drive in any other way than risky. When I have to surpass the limit, I do it. Every driver has a limit, mine is just a little further."

- Lewis Hamilton: "I don't aspire to be like other drivers, I aspire to be unique in my own way."

97

Famous quotes.

- Nelson Piquet: "Driving in Monaco is like riding a bike inside a house."

- James Hunt: "Sex is my best training."

- Niki Lauda: "A wise man gets more from his enemies than a fool from his friends."

- Ayrton Senna: "Second place is the first of the losers."

- Lewis Hamilton: "If you don't have the balls to brake late, it's your problem."

- Juan Manuel Fangio: "Races are not won in the first corner. Many times they are lost."

96

Famous quotes.

- James Hunt: "I live fast because I know that on the track, I can die in a second."

- Lewis Hamilton: "I think taking more risks is what sets apart the faster drivers from the maybe not-so-fast ones."

- Niki Lauda: "You don't have to talk too much, just focus on your goal and achieve it."

- Juan Manuel Fangio: "Races are not won in the first corner. Many times they are lost."

- Ayrton Senna: "There is no corner where overtaking is impossible. It's just a matter of deciding the best moment to do it."

95

6 Famous quotes.

- Juan Manuel Fangio: "Excessive slowness is also a risk. Beware of becoming a hindrance on the road or in life."

- Ayrton Senna: "We can push to the limit and enjoy it at the same time."

- Niki Lauda: "The only charisma a guy like Lewis Hamilton has is his girlfriend."

- Alain Prost, 1984: "When everything is going smoothly, I get bored."

- Ayrton Senna, 1993: "Superstitions? I don't believe in them, I only believe in work."

- James Hunt: "It's true that sometimes I would vomit before races, but not because I was afraid of the risk I was going to take, but because of the fear of failure, of not performing well in the race."

94

6 Famous quotes.

- Jean Alesi: "To be honest, when I was a kid, I never thought I would make it to F1. I always believed it was too difficult for me, and that only the greatest, like Gilles Villeneuve, could achieve it."

- Derek Warwick (In 1990, about his experience with bad cars, with which he achieved better results than expected): "People don't realize, but winning a race is often easier than finishing seventh. Finishing seventh can be torture if the car you're driving is not meant to be there."

- Ayrton Senna, 1983: "When records are broken, it doesn't mean you are the best; it's difficult to compare drivers who haven't competed against each other. For me, each race is different, and I only aim to gain experience and build my personality so that when the time comes to step up to F1, which is an important step, I have enough experience and confidence to succeed."

- Niki Lauda: "Alain Prost was a dog, but Fernando Alonso is much worse."

- Ayrton Senna: "The pole position is the final sprint. The driver must summon all their qualities: experience, instinct, aggression, calculation. And use them at an extremely high level. Racing for pole is giving it your all, and I love that."

- Juan Manuel Fangio: "To win, the first thing you have to do is finish."

93

6 Famous quotes.

- Sebastian Vettel (in response to media questions about his sporting ambitions after winning his third world title, February 2013): "World domination? I'm German, so I wouldn't say that. Besides, I don't have a mustache either."

- Fernando Alonso, April 2014: "I have hunger for victory, hunger for success, and I'll tell you that two titles are not enough."

- Daniel Ricciardo (explaining why he has had better luck with his car than Sebastian Vettel, July 2014): "The secret? I give mine a kiss every night, with tongue."

- Jacques Villeneuve (showing that he still hadn't figured out why Michael Schumacher had returned to competition, March 2011): "What is his real motivation? Last year, he was smiling even after a bad result."

- Ayrton Senna: "I am truly privileged. I always had a very good life, but everything I achieved was through dedication, perseverance, and a strong desire to fulfill my goals and many desires for victory in life, not just victory as a driver. Whatever you do now, whoever you are and whatever position you have, whether it's at a high level or a lower level, achieve your goals with great strength and determination, and always do everything with love and strong faith in God, because someday you will reach Him, you will somehow reach Him."

- Niki Lauda: "I am ugly because I had an accident; most people don't have an excuse."

92

6 Famous quotes.

- Jenson Button, May 2011: "The day I stop driving for McLaren will be the day I hang up my gloves."

- Niki Lauda: "The only important victory in this business is the day you leave the paddock alive."

- Ted Kravitz from Sky Sports, February 2013: "Everyone has new cars. Now they have to check if the brakes work."

- Hermann Tilke, 2012: "In the end, overtaking is only possible if there is a faster driver behind and a slower driver ahead. If the opposite happens, then..."

- Ayrton Senna, 1991: "We only take more risks than people in other professions, and that's why we handle fear better."

- Juan Manuel Fangio: "You should always try to be the best, but never believe you are the best."

91

6 Famous quotes.

- Alain Prost, 1984: "There is nothing natural in F1, and I can't stand the artificiality."

- Flavio Briatore, 1996: "I never believe anything that is said in F1."

- Elio de Angelis, 1985: "Long ago, my father asked me why I had a tendency to do things in the most complicated way. My response was, 'Difficulty makes you desire things more'."

- Stirling Moss, 1994: "There are two things a man will never say he can do well at the same time: drive and make love."

- Ayrton Senna (to journalists after winning at Interlagos in 1991): "When God wants something, no one can oppose Him."

- Niki Lauda: "You don't learn anything from success. You do learn from mistakes and problems."

90

6 Famous quotes.

- John Watson: "A driver is an artist, and driving is an expression of myself. This is not a job, but a definition of who I am."

- Alan Jones, 1980: "Driving at the limit is a matter of trust. If you have it, you can do anything. If not, you're nothing."

- Niki Lauda: "Even a chimpanzee could drive today's Formula 1 cars."

- Mario Andretti, 1990: "You always see gaps during the races. You just have to make sure they're bigger than your car."

- Ayrton Senna (in response to Ferrari's offer to race for them, 1992): "I race to win championships, not to make money..."

- James Hunt: "You shouldn't worry about your face, Niki, you were ugly before the accident."

89

6 Funny quotes from pilots.

- Andrea De Adamich: "Andrea Moreno is doing very well, he's already on Berger's ass."

- Scirio: "But if a Formula 1 driver finishes first in every race... do they win the Grand Prix?"

- Michelle Hunziker: "Why does Schumacher always win? Because he practices in the... chin gallery."

- Marco Della Noce: "Barrichello: a genetically modified Brazilian, he likes to browse Luca Cordero di Montezemolo's boxers."

- Marco Della Noce: "At Ferrari, we're a great team that makes no distinction between the drivers. To enter the pit lane, we gave Soccmaker the remote control; Irvine has to get out and ring the bell."

- Ayrton Senna: "My goal is to brake, always, right after the marks left by the other drivers."

88

Normal cars are better: 7 reasons.

- No headlights: No wonder they only drive during the day.

- Only one brake light: Countless accidents every year to report to the insurance.

- Only one seat: How can a guy make out with his girlfriend at the local drive-in theater?

- No anchor for a baby seat: And they're trying to make us believe that safety comes first?

- No adjustable seats: Very uncomfortable (my seat goes forward and backward, and it can also recline)

- High fuel consumption: You have to choose between feeding the car or your kids.

- Engines and tires that don't last: After 5-6 races with your friends, you have to spend a lot of money to replace them, and there are no 2-for-1 deals.

87

Normal cars are better: 8 reasons

- No doors: Anyone can get in and steal it.

- No roof: People driving these things are exposed to the elements. Even convertibles have something you can put over your head.

- No radio (AM and FM), no cassette or CD player, MP3...: How boring must it be to drive in those things for almost 2 hours without having anything to listen to.

- No heating: By leaving them exposed to the elements, the driver's toes must freeze like ice cubes in no time.

- No coffee cup holders: The driver can spill hot things like coffee, waffles, and other dangerous things like moving your entire house on themselves.

- No ashtrays and electric lighters...: There are no words to describe such horror.

- No windshield wipers: And they expect them to race in the rain?

- No turn signals: How can they indicate their intention to overtake or change direction?

86

Piquet to Mansell: The best on paper.

Nelson Piquet and Nigel Mansell were teammates in 1986 and 1987 at Williams Honda, which was the best car at the time.

The penultimate race of their collaboration was the Mexican Grand Prix.

During practice, the Brazilian noticed that the British driver was stopping too frequently due to intestinal problems.

So he decided to remove the toilet paper from all the toilets, but his colleague didn't notice until he was already seated.

It is said that he reacted with the roar of a lion, fitting for his nickname.

85

Lauda to a journalist: Don't look at me,
I can't hear you.

Despite the pain he suffered from his accident at
the old Nurburgring, the late Niki Lauda was a
spirited man and was the first to win a world
championship with Brembo brakes.

On the occasion of the premiere of the movie Rush,
he returned to the site of the accident,
at the Bergwerk corner, with an American
television crew.

When the reporter asked him how he felt,
he started talking, then looked down at the
grass and picked something up, saying,
"Look what's there! It's my ear."

The cameraman and the woman
were left speechless.

In reality, he was holding a cookie
that he had hidden earlier.

84

Pérez to his engineers: We need to talk when I come back.

In 2011, Sergio Pérez made his Formula 1 debut with the Sauber team powered by Ferrari.

During the first 14 races, he had scored points only three times.

In Japan, thanks to two pit stops and judicious tire management, the Mexican driver managed to climb to eighth place on lap 42, but on the final lap, he started shouting over the radio, "I have no power, I have no power," which confused everyone.

Crossing the finish line in 8th position, he burst into laughter: "Ha, ha, ha, I was just kidding."

83

Berger to Senna: It's always about jumps.

Gerhard Berger is the driver who spent the most time with Ayrton Senna: together, they competed in the McLaren equipped with Brembo brakes for three seasons, from 1990 to 1992, a total of forty-eight Grand Prix races.

Their understanding was evident, even to the least observant, and they left us with many anecdotes.

One day, during a helicopter flight not far from the Monza circuit, the Austrian threw Senna's carbon fiber briefcase, claiming it was indestructible.

Nobody has forgotten that famous trip to Australia where he released a dozen frogs in his hotel room.

82

Monaco to change its circuit to allow more overtaking in 2021.

Monaco will introduce the changes needed for F1 to finally be exciting: jump platforms, dash panels, and even fire!

(April Fool's Day prank from 2021)

81

The FIA will disqualify anyone who exceeds track limits at Imola.

Following the inconsistency with track limits at Turn 4 in Bahrain, the FIA will be much stricter at Imola.

Any driver who exceeds the limits will be disqualified.

A driver who goes off track during practice sessions will not be allowed to race for the rest of the event.

(April Fool's Day prank from 2021)

80

Max Verstappen allowed to use alternative layout at Zandvoort.

Red Bull driver will have the opportunity to use a different design for his home Grand Prix.

"For Max, we will install a different version of the Audi chicane in the second half of the lap," announced Jan Lammers, sporting director of the Dutch Grand Prix, as reported by F1 Insider.

"We saw in Bahrain how carrying more speed through Turn 4 on 29 occasions helped Lewis Hamilton keep our lion at bay more than he might have on a regular track, so we are confident that this faster version in one of our tightest sectors will give Max the help he needs to win and give our incredible fans exactly what they want to see," Lammers added.

(April Fool's Day prank from 2021).

79

Drawing of Alonso for sale
with cryptocurrencies:

A drawing of the Spanish driver
called "El Matador di Catalonia"
is being auctioned and can be
purchased with cryptocurrencies.

(April Fool's Day prank from 2021)

78

Magnussen to replace Mazepin starting from Imola.

The Danish newspaper Bil claims that Magnussen is returning to his former team to replace Nikita Mazepin.

They point out that the Russian driver has not impressed in his first Formula 1 weekend, and the American outfit is bringing back Kevin.

(April Fool's Day prank from 2021)

77

Mercedes appoints special advisor to one of its photographers.

The German team has issued a detailed statement announcing that they have appointed one of their photographers, Paul Ripke, as a special advisor to the team.

"Mercedes strengthens its future with a strategic change within the organization. We announce an appointment as part of the long-term plan to continuously grow both on and off the track. With immediate effect, the team appoints Paul Ripke as a special advisor, a new position that will work in coordination with Toto Wolff."

"It's a dream come true," Ripke says.

"When Paul started attending the engineers' meetings, he provided valuable content and quickly earned a seat at our table," Wolff shares.

A prank pulled by Mercedes on April 1, 2019.

76

Nico Rosberg returns to Formula 1 in 2020.

"I announce my return to Formula 1 in 2020," the German titled in the videoblog he posted on YouTube, where he recaps the Bahrain race.

"Sorry, guys, it's April Fool's Day. I couldn't resist. I had to put that title. I'm sorry it's not true, I know many of you would have liked it, but I definitely won't be coming back."

75

Formula 1 to use nuclear-electric engines in 2024.

This news was posted on Twitter by Formula E driver Di Grassi, along with the message.

"What? Incredible!"

74

Red Bull buys Rich Energy.

The website F1i.com published the prank that Red Bull co-founder Dietrich Mateschitz purchased Rich Energy.

"The move by the beverage company is surprising given the insignificant sales of the Rich Energy product, which are nearly invisible in the market."

Thus, Red Bull expands its presence in Formula 1 to a third team.

"Rich Energy caught my interest when its owner, Storey, said they aimed to beat Red Bull both on and off the track."

I wondered, "What does this man drink to say such things?" says Mateschitz, according to this fictional news.

73

Formula 1 creates a parallel
category for dogs.

In honor of their recent collaboration with
The Chemical Brothers, the Grand Circus
has decided to play a prank.

They have introduced the "F1 Dog," featuring
a grid with 20 dogs and 20 new circuits.

Among them will be Max Fetchstappen, a
desperate red pit bull determined to be the
top dog, the energetic Charles Leclerc King
Charles Spaniel, and the water dog Ricciardo,
known as "a good boy."

They have also announced that instead of
racing in Baku, they will compete in "Barku,"
as "bark" means "to bark" in Spanish.

"Faster, fiercer, and more hairy" is the
slogan for this category.

72

Ferrari and Vettel part ways
by mutual agreement.

Statement: Ferrari explains that
after the disaster in Bahrain,
the German will no longer work
for the Scuderia.

The team replaces him with
Kimi Räikkönen.

– The French publication
Auto Hebdo made it up.

71

A Formula 1 driver is sleeping when suddenly
he wakes up with a jolt.

He asks, "What's happening?"

His mechanic responds, "You were dreaming about
the track, and you turned the steering
wheel by accident."

A while later, another jolt.

The driver asks again, "What's happening now?"

The mechanic replies, "You're still dreaming,
this time you accidentally hit the accelerator."

The driver, a bit more alert, asks, "What if
I wake up and really accelerate?"

His mechanic answers, "Don't worry,
I have the handbrake on."

70

What does Wurz do
when he picks
his nose?

He brings out the
best in himself.

69

Dear Abby, I've never written to you before,
but I really need your advice.

I have long suspected that my wife is cheating
on me with a Formula 1 driver.

The usual signs are there.

She's always talking about her time at the circuits, but
whenever I ask her the name of the driver, she always says,
"Oh, he's just a friend from the track, you don't know him."

I always try to stay awake and watch for her arrival home
after a race, but I usually end up falling asleep.

Anyway, I've never confronted the issue with my wife.

I think deep down I didn't want to know the truth, but last
night she went out again, and I decided to really check it out.

Around midnight, I decided to hide in the garage behind my
race car so I could have a good view of the street when she
came home from a night at the paddock.

It was at that moment, crouched behind my car, that I noticed
one of the tires seemed to have a crack right along the edge.

Is this something I can fix myself, or should I take
it to the team of mechanics?

68

Lewis Hamilton is driving his Mercedes on the race track at 300 km/h.

A skateboarder is riding next to him.

Hamilton thinks, "I have to go faster!"

So, he accelerates to 350 km/h.

The skateboarder keeps up with him.

Hamilton accelerates to 400 km/h, but the skateboarder is still right beside him.

Hamilton leans over and asks, "How are you doing that?"

The skateboarder replies, "It's simple, I have a 150-kilogram V6 hybrid engine with 900 horsepower on my skateboard."

67

Why can't Formula 1
drivers be good
bus drivers?

Because they always
want to overtake
everyone else.

66

A penguin and a cat meet each other.

The penguin says, "Do you know who I am?"

The cat responds, "Yes, you're the penguin!"

But do you know who I am?"

The penguin considers it and says, "No wings, no engine, you could be Lewis Hamilton!"

65

Why are Formula 1
drivers always in
a bad mood?

Because they're
always revved up.

64

A dog and a bird meet each other.

The dog says, "Do you
know who I am?"

The bird responds,
"Yes, you're the dog!"

But do you know who I am?"

The dog considers it and says,
"No wheels, no engine, you could
be Sebastian Vettel!"

63

A man walks into a bar and says to the bartender, "I want a martini, but no olives."

The bartender replies, "Are you a Formula 1 driver?"

The man asks, "How did you know?"

The bartender says, "Because all Formula 1 drivers want their martinis without obstacles."

62

What is written on the
back of Wurz's car?

"I also brake
for Austria!"

61

Lewis Hamilton and Max Verstappen are competing in a Formula 1 race.

Max says to Lewis, "I'm going to overtake you in the next corner."

Lewis responds, "Good luck with that, the last time I tried to overtake myself, I ended up hitting the wall."

60

A Formula 1 driver is practicing on a circuit.

Suddenly, a man runs up to him and says, "Stop, stop! There's a bee in your car."

The driver stops the vehicle and asks, "Where is the bee?"

The man replies, "I don't know, but you were driving so fast, I thought you might be taking it with you."

59

Why did Mercedes
hire Wurz?

Nobody knows, not even
the executives, but it
is speculated that the
purpose was to distract
from the A-Class.

58

One woman asks another, "What do you prefer, your husband racing in Formula 1 or having a relationship with another woman?"

And she responds, "Having a relationship with another woman."

Surprised, her friend asks, "Why do you prefer that?"

She answers, "Because at least he won't be talking about his track time all day long."

57

A Formula 1 driver is in his car before
a race, and right next to the circuit,
there is a funeral taking place.

The driver interrupts his concentration,
pauses for a moment to observe the
funeral, bows as a sign of respect,
and returns to his car.

His mechanic says, "You are a very noble
person, feeling the pain of others when
they lose a loved one. I am proud to
work with you."

The driver replies, "Well, it's the least I
could do; we were married for 25 years."

56

What do Michael Schumacher and Harald Juhnke have in common?

They both can't get past a Williams.

55

A journalist from a women's magazine asks Formula 1 world champion Villeneuve what he thinks of German top models.

He smiles and says, "Better with Claudia Schiffer in a four-poster bed than with Michael Schumacher in a gravel bed!"

54

Michael Schumacher is driving his Ferrari on the highway at 250 km/h.

A moped is driving next to him.

Schumacher thinks, "I have to be faster!"

So, he accelerates to 330 km/h.

The moped is still driving alongside him.

Schumi accelerates to 370 km/h.

But the moped is still driving next to him.

Schumacher rolls down the window and asks, "Is there a tiger in the tank?"

"No! The jacket is on the door!"

53

What's the difference between Siegfried & Roy and the Schuhmacher brothers?

The facial expression when one pushes the other from behind!

52

After an epic race on the track, the drivers decide to relax at the circuit's bar.

While having a drink, one of them comments, "You know what has really made the difference in this race? The ability to take high-speed turns without going off the track."

Another driver responds, "That's easy, you just need a good car and a great team."

The first driver smiles and says, "But it also helps if you're Michael Schumacher's son."

The second driver raises an eyebrow and says, "Oh, are you Michael Schumacher's son?"

The first driver replies, "No, but I'd like to believe I am."

51

What thoughts does a
Formula 1 driver have
before the corner?

Does the mechanic
know I'm with his wife?

50

One day, Hamilton and Verstappen
go to a racing store.

Hamilton looks at the first car and says,
"This is the best, I want it."

The salesman responds, "That's a Mercedes,
one of the best cars on the track."

Verstappen looks at the second car and says,
"This is the best, I want it."

The salesman replies, "That's a Red Bull, with
impressive performance and agile handling."

Finally, the salesman asks them, "And what
do you think of the third car?"

Hamilton and Verstappen look and say in
unison, "That's a Ferrari, too slow for us!"

49

An elephant and a snake meet.

The elephant says, "Do you know who I am?"

The snake replies, "Yes, the elephant! But do you also know who I am?"

The elephant considers it and says, "Bald, no ears... you could be Nicki Lauda!"

48

One day, a Formula 1 driver arrived at the track and found a mechanic working on his car.

"What are you doing?" the driver asked.

"I'm fixing the braking system," replied the mechanic.

"That's great!" exclaimed the driver.

"Why didn't you do it before the last race?"

47

Hamilton, Vettel, and Alonso are in heaven, and God tells them that one of them must become His celestial race driver.

Vettel says, "I have won 4 championships and have driven for Ferrari."

Alonso replies, "But I have two championships and have won with different teams and different types of cars."

Then, Hamilton looks at God and says, "God, you're sitting in my seat."

46

What do you call a lap where Wurz is not overtaken?

Pace car phase.

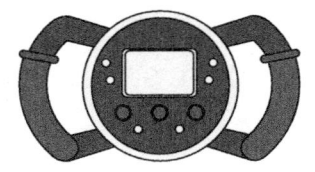

45

Why did Villeneuve
allow 2 Mercedes to
overtake him just
before the finish line
in the last Formula 1
race in 1997?

He was afraid they
would fall on top of him.

44

Robert Kubica encounters a genie who grants him three wishes.

Kubica reflects and says, "I want to be the fastest driver in the world, have an indestructible car, and win every race."

The genie replies, "That sounds good, but what about the enjoyment that competition brings?"

The driver responds with a smile, "Oh, let that be for the other drivers."

43

A young boy finally managed to get the prettiest girl in high school to go out with him.

So, he takes her to a nightclub on a Saturday night, and then, during the course of the night, he convinces her to join him and spend some time in the car.

That's when things start to get steamy, except the girl immediately tells him, "You know, I'm still a virgin and I want to stay that way!"

The guy brazenly replies, "Well, it doesn't matter. Will you give me a lollipop?"

"Hey, no way! I'm not putting your thing in my mouth!"

A bit discouraged, the guy persists, "How about a hand job then?"

"I've never done that. Tell me how it goes..."

"Well, it's quite simple. If you look at Formula 1 drivers, when they've won a race, they go up on the podium, and then they're given a bottle of champagne that they shake to spray everyone around... Well, the same thing happens with a hand job."

Then the girl responds that it's "fine," unbuttons his pants, and takes out his joystick, then she starts giving it the appropriate back-and-forth motion at an increasingly higher frequency.

A few seconds later, the guy drops his head on the headrest, his eyes close, his legs stiffen... he's surely about to climax... but instead, he lets out a heartbreaking scream of pain, "OHHHHHHH!"

The girl panics and stops to ask, "What's wrong? What did I do wrong?"
"Take your thumb off the end!"

42

Ferrari F1 fired their entire Pit Stop team yesterday.

The announcement came after Ferrari decided to take advantage of the government law to hire unemployed youths from Naples.

The decision to hire them came after a recent investigation into the ability of unemployed Neapolitan youths to remove a set of wheels from a car in less than 6 seconds without the proper equipment, while Ferrari's current crew can only do it in 8 seconds and with technological equipment costing millions of euros.

Consider this an excellent and bold move by the Ferrari F1 team, as most races are won or lost in Pit Stops.

Ferrari would thus have an advantage over all other teams in the world championship.

Today, during the crew's first practice session, the Neapolitans not only managed to change the tires in less than 6 seconds, but in 12 seconds, they also repainted, registered, and sold the car to McLaren for four boxes of cigarettes.

41

What happens if
Alexander Wurz presses
the speed limiter when
entering the pit lane?

The rear wheels of his
Benetton start spinning!

40

One fine day, Moses, Jesus Christ, and a retired driver are racing in a Formula 1 race.

Suddenly, Moses prepares himself and boom, his car goes straight into the water.

Everyone exclaims, "Oh no!"

But Moses says, "No worries."

He takes a staff, sticks it into the ground, and the waters part, revealing a path to the track.

He hits the accelerator and overtakes all the other racers except Jesus Christ and the retired driver.

The crowd goes wild.

Next, Jesus Christ takes a turn and boom, his car goes straight into the water, but this time it floats on top of it.

Jesus Christ keeps control and gains a significant lead.

Finally, the retired driver prepares himself and boom, his car goes straight into the water, but just before reaching it, a mechanic comes out with a boat and rescues him, leaving him near the finish line, allowing him to win.

The crowd is amazed, but the retired driver explains, "I have many friends in the pit lane."

39

The performance of the car intended for the upcoming Formula 1 championship, known as the Ferrari named after Gianni Agnelli, was immediately notable: the car's strong point seems to be its traction, confirming once again the old popular saying "a strand of a woman's hair pulls more than a thick ship's rope."

38

What would happen if all the drivers, except Alexander Wurz, retired from an F1 race?

Wurz would be the first driver to win a Formula 1 race and a 24-hour race at the same time!

37

Year 1983.

A Sicilian Ferrari club goes to Monza to attend the Formula 1 Grand Prix; they enter the racetrack, the party led by Ninetto (named so because of his short stature) settles in a grandstand filled with fans of the Cavallino Rampante from Maranello.

Ninetto, overwhelmed by the crowd, tries to understand the progress of the race, but jubilation is everywhere; he asks to the right, asks to the left, but no one listens.

Thus, the race ends, with people parading disappointed by Ferrari's non-victory.

Ninetto finds his friend Salvatore and asks him, "Totò, can you tell me who won?"

And his friend, sadly, says, "Piquet..." Ninetto concludes, "Why the hell didn't I see anything?!"

36

A Formula 1 driver encounters a fan
in the paddock before the race.

"How do you plan to win this race?"
the fan asks.

"Well, I'm going to accelerate
and turn in the corners,"
the driver responds.

"Is that all?" the fan asks, surprised.

"Yes, that's all," the driver
replies with a smile.

"But you have to do it very fast."

35

Michael Schumacher's wife tells him that she doesn't want turkey for Christmas this year.

Michael, somewhat surprised, replies, "How about if I buy you Denmark instead?"

34

Years ago, Alexander Wurz was walking down a street in a small Austrian village.

Then he saw a very old woman walking very slowly, apparently in some pain while walking.

Alex, being a very polite young man, stops his car, rolls down the window, and asks, "Ma'am, would you like me to give you a ride?"

She looks at him pleasantly surprised but suddenly recognizes him and says, "Oh, no, thank you, I'm in a hurry!"

33

A couple is in bed, and the phone rings.

The woman answers it.

"Oh, yes, have fun!"

"Who was it?"

"My husband, he says he's with you watching the Formula 1 race."

32

Schumacher and Barrichello went fishing.

While sitting on the riverbank, Rubens says, "The last time I was here, I caught a fish this big," and he showed the size with one hand on the other forearm.

Schumacher looks at his forearm thoughtfully for several seconds and then bursts out laughing, "Rubens, you must be joking. That hairy fish doesn't exist."

31

One day, a Formula 1 driver met an elderly man at a bar.

The old man asked him how he got started in Formula 1 racing.

The driver replied, "Well, it all started when I was a child and used to race my bike down the hills near my home. I loved the feeling of speed and freedom I had while pedaling."

The old man nodded and said, "Yes, I remember that feeling. But how did you go from racing on a bicycle to racing in a Formula 1 car?"

The driver smiled and answered, "Well, one day I just got tired of having to pedal so much."

30

Hamilton and Verstappen go to a bar.

The bartender asks them what they would like to drink.

Hamilton says, "Give me a martini, shaken, not stirred."

Verstappen replies, "Just give me a beer, no frills here."

The bartender serves them their drinks and asks about their occupation.

Hamilton responds, "I'm a Formula 1 driver."

Verstappen adds, "And so am I."

The bartender is surprised, "Do you really race together in the same race?"

Hamilton nods, "Yes, but I always finish ahead."

Verstappen smiles and says, "But I always have more fun on the track."

29

What slogan do you
get when you combine
Star Wars and F1?

"May the aerodynamic
downforce be
with you."

28

Vettel and Alonso are in a desert.

Evening comes, and they set up their tent.

Both go to sleep.

Alonso wakes up in the middle of the night.

Vettel is not in the tent.

He can hear something coming from outside the tent.

Alonso peeks out and sees Vettel running around the tent like crazy, with a big lion chasing him...

Alonso shouts, "Run faster, it's going to catch you!"

Vettel replies, "Don't worry, I'm leading by three laps."

27

Why is the F1 mascot named Lewis?

Because he's always on pole position.

26

What's the advantage if Wurz doesn't compete in F1 races?

Heinz Peter Prüller lives longer.

25

"You're late to the tee, John."

"Yeah, well, being Sunday,
I had to flip a coin to see if
I should go to church or
watch the race."

"Alright, but why are
you so late?"

"I had to flip it 15 times!"

24

In 1988, Enzo Anselmo Ferrari dies after
living a fulfilling life.

When he arrived in heaven, God showed him around.

They came to a modest little house with a small
Ferrari flag in the window.

"This house is yours for eternity, Enzo," said God.

"This is very special, not everyone has a house here."

Enzo felt special and walked up to his house.

As he stood on the porch, he spotted another
house around the corner.

It was a huge mansion with a carbon fiber sidewalk,
a 50-foot flagpole with a giant Porsche flag,
and a Porsche emblem on every window.

Enzo looked at God and said, "God, I don't mean to be
ungrateful, but I have a great manufacturer; my cars won
Le Mans and F1 championships. Why does Ferdinand
Porsche have a better house than me?"

God chuckled and said, "Enzo, that's not
Ferdinand's house, it's mine!"

23

Xandl says to Briatore, "I will make you the happiest team boss in Formula 1, I promise!"

Briatore responds, "I will miss you, Alex!"

22

A Mercedes driver, a Ferrari driver, and
a Red Bull driver walk into a bar.

They start talking, and after a few drinks,
the conversation shifts to cars.

The Mercedes driver, known for his consistency
and efficiency, only has a sedan.

The other two laugh at him, saying
he has a bad car.

The Ferrari driver, known for his passion and
skill on the track, shows off his sports car.

The customers in the bar are amazed, and even the
Mercedes driver has to admit it's a good vehicle.

The Red Bull driver leaves, goes around the corner,
and after a few minutes, comes back flying
through the air with his jetpack and
blows up the other cars.

He has the speed and the most
advanced technology.

21

Wurz rarely has an engine failure; instead, his engine often dies while it's running.

20

"You spend too much time thinking about Formula 1!"

"Do you remember the day we got married?"

"Of course I do!"

"It was the same day Max Verstappen won the United States Grand Prix."

19

Why do Formula 1
drivers wear
fireproof suits?

Because they like
to feel the burn
of speed.

18

Lewis Hamilton and Max Verstappen are in a Formula 1 race.

Max Verstappen starts overtaking Lewis with his fast pace.

Lewis feels threatened and says to his engineer, "What's wrong with my car? Why is Verstappen so fast?"

The engineer replies, "It's not your car, Lewis. It's the driver."

17

A Formula 1 driver was on the starting grid before a race.

He turned to his mechanic and said, "How fast is this car?"

The mechanic replied, "Fast enough to win the race, but not fast enough to avoid a crash."

The driver responded, "Well, I hope you're right about the first part."

16

What are the sponsor logos on Xandl's car called?

Covert advertising.

15

A Formula 1 fan meets up with a friend at a bar and starts talking about their love for the sport.

"There's nothing like watching those drivers racing at high speeds and competing for victory," says the fan.

His friend asks, "What about the sound of the engine and the excitement of the game?"

The fan responds, "Oh, that's secondary. What I really enjoy is seeing the sponsors on the cars."

His friend looks at him oddly and says, "You mean you like seeing ads in the middle of a race?"

The fan shrugs and replies, "Well, someone has to pay for those tires."

14

Lewis Hamilton and Max Verstappen
are in a bar after a race.

Lewis says, "Have you seen how
I overtook everyone today
on the track?"

Max replies, "Yes, I saw how you
overtook everyone, except me."

Lewis asks, "How did you do it?"

Max answers, "Simple, I just
accelerated a little bit more."

13

What does Ron Dennis do with his rear end in the morning?

He instructs it and sends it to the test track in last year's car.

12

A Formula 1 driver approaches his mechanic and says, "I need my car to go faster to win tomorrow's race."

The mechanic replies, "No problem, you just need to learn to keep your head down and your foot on the accelerator."

The driver asks, "Isn't there anything else you can do to improve the car's performance?"

The mechanic responds, "Well, we can try asking Lewis Hamilton to drive it for you."

11

Attention:

Benetton is planning a sensational driver change for the next season: Alex Wurz will be replaced by Frank Williams.

In secret driving tests, Williams was 3 tenths faster in a wheelchair than Wurz!

10

One day, a Formula 1 driver encountered a fan in the pit lane.

The fan asked how he could improve his lap time on the track.

The driver responded, "Well, the first thing you need is a good car. Then, you need a good team of mechanics to ensure your car is in good condition, and finally, you need a good driver to harness all that potential."

The fan thought about this for a moment and then asked, "What if I don't have any of those?"

The driver smiled and replied, "Well, then you'll have to buy a ticket and enjoy the race like any other spectator."

9

The Pope and the Prime Minister of Israel decide to have
a Formula 1 race to demonstrate their friendship
and sportsmanship.

The Pope is concerned about his lack of racing skills, but
one of the cardinals suggests they get Lewis Hamilton,
a devout Catholic and Formula 1 champion,
to represent him.

Hamilton agrees and takes to the track
to represent the Pope.

After an intense race, Hamilton calls the Vatican
to report the results.

"It's Lewis Hamilton, Your Holiness," says the driver.

"I have good news and bad news."

"Tell me the good news, Lewis," the Pope responds.

"The good news, Your Holiness, is that I was truly
inspired in the race and drove like never before. It was
a truly miraculous race," says Hamilton.

"And the bad news?" the Pope asks.

"I lost by a crushing margin to Rabbi Sebastian Vettel,"
Hamilton replies with a sigh.

8

Why do Formula 1 drivers always wear gloves?

Because it's easier to accelerate with a soft grip.

7

A woman says, "I don't mind us buying the second Ferrari, having our apartment and house painted red, nor do I mind the bedsheets being red, you always dressing in the same color, vacations in Italy, it doesn't matter. But naming our two daughters Michael and Ralf is going too far."

6

Why do Formula 1
drivers always
wear helmets?

Because if they
didn't, their brains
would fly out
at 300 km/h.

5

How do you know when a Formula 1 driver is getting old?

When they start complaining that the current cars are too fast and lack the class of the old ones.

4

Wurz is driving a fast race for him when suddenly he sees Bernoldi approaching in the rearview mirror.

He's getting closer and closer.

Wurz accelerates, and Bernoldi gets even closer.

He's now driving alongside Wurz.

Wurz looks at him and hears Bernoldi shout, "Hey, snail, help me out, I'm new here, where's the second course?"

3

On a Sunday, after the church service, one of the parishioners approached the priest and asked, "Reverend, is it a sin to race on the circuit on Sundays?"

"My child," said the priest, placing his hand on his shoulder, "I've seen you drive, and in your case, it's a sin any day."

2

A Formula 1 driver ran into a friend who worked as a mechanic at a small car repair shop.

The friend asked how it was to compete in Formula 1.

The driver responded, "It's an emotional rollercoaster. One moment you're at the top, with maximum speed and adrenaline rushing through your veins, and the next moment, you're struggling to maintain control when things go wrong."

The mechanic nodded and replied, "Well, sounds like any day at the workshop."

1

Schumacher and Barrichello were competing on a go-kart track.

After the race, Barrichello boasted about his ability to overtake Schumacher.

Schumacher smiled and replied, "Sure, you've always been good at overtaking on the straightaways, but have you ever tried completing a whole lap?"

FORMULA 1
JOKES

JOKES, FAMOUS QUOTES,
AND FUNNY ANECDOTES.

Original Title: FORMULA 1 JOKES.

© FORMULA 1 JOKES, Carlos Martínez Cerdá and Víctor Martínez Cerdá, 2023

Authors: Víctor Martínez Cerdá and Carlos Martínez Cerdá (V&C Brothers)

© Cover and illustrations: V&C Brothers

Layout and design: V&C Brothers